Air Sovereignty

Johanna Francina Lycklama

The Making of Modern Law collection of legal archives constitutes a genuine revolution in historical legal research because it opens up a wealth of rare and previously inaccessible sources in legal, constitutional, administrative, political, cultural, intellectual, and social history. This unique collection consists of three extensive archives that provide insight into more than 300 years of American and British history. These collections include:

Legal Treatises, 1800-1926: over 20,000 legal treatises provide a comprehensive collection in legal history, business and economics, politics and government.

Trials, 1600-1926: nearly 10,000 titles reveal the drama of famous, infamous, and obscure courtroom cases in America and the British Empire across three centuries.

Primary Sources, 1620-1926: includes reports, statutes and regulations in American history, including early state codes, municipal ordinances, constitutional conventions and compilations, and law dictionaries.

These archives provide a unique research tool for tracking the development of our modern legal system and how it has affected our culture, government, business – nearly every aspect of our everyday life. For the first time, these high-quality digital scans of original works are available via print-on-demand, making them readily accessible to libraries, students, independent scholars, and readers of all ages.

GUIDE TO FOLD-OUTS MAPS and OVERSIZED IMAGES

The book you are reading was digitized from microfilm captured over the past thirty to forty years. Years after the creation of the original microfilm, the book was converted to digital files and made available in an online database.

In an online database, page images do not need to conform to the size restrictions found in a printed book. When converting these images back into a printed bound book, the page sizes are standardized in ways that maintain the detail of the original. For large images, such as fold-out maps, the original page image is split into two or more pages

Guidelines used to determine how to split the page image follows:

• Some images are split vertically; large images require vertical and horizontal splits.
• For horizontal splits, the content is split left to right.
• For vertical splits, the content is split from top to bottom.
• For both vertical and horizontal splits, the image is processed from top left to bottom right.

AIR SOVEREIGNTY

AIR SOVEREIGNTY

BY

Dr. J. F. LYCKLAMA à NIJEHOLT

THE HAGUE

MARTINUS NIJHOFF

1910

PRINTED BY KOCH & KNUTTEL — GOUDA

CONTENTS.

CONSEQUENCES OF THE SOVEREIGNTY THEORY.

APPENDICES.

INTRODUCTION.

Whilst the technical expert from one century to another was engaged in investigating the problem of the navigation of the air, the jurist could afford to look on calm and unmoved as one experiment after another failed. Even the indications of future success, such as Liliënthal's successful floating experiments and the fact of the airship of Renard-Krebs succeeding in returning to its startingpoint, were insufficient to set the jurist to work; for him it is unnecessary to make a beginning until the preparative task of the technical expert has been successfully achieved. So long as there were available only undirigible balloons, dangerous and expensive, absolutely unfit for regular traffic, aerial navigation was therefore necessarily confined to some very unfrequent ascents, such as attractions at exhibitions, for pleasure trips or scientific excursions and most occasionally for military purposes; it did not create situations and relationships demanding the immediate attention of the legislator. We find a single exception though in the case of the escapes by balloon from Paris during the siege of 1870, which gave occasion to Bismarck's considering all aeronauts as spies. Bismarck's view of the matter was disapproved of by the Brussels Conference for international law of 1874, and by the Hague Peace Conferences, both of 1899 and of 1907, and led to the rule that such aeronauts as bear dispatches or maintain the communication between different parts of the army or the country, are not subject to the charge of espionage 1). It is not to be denied that this rule goes too far in following

---

1) Brussels Declarations 1874, art. 22.
Convention concerning the laws and customs of land warfare, art. 29. Peace Conf. 1899 and 1907.

1

secrecy nor pretence is possible! No doubt it is but reasonable only to exempt them under the same conditions as are required for their terrestrial colleagues' exemption, namely that they performed the said actions openly.

It is but natural that the drawing nearer to technical aeronautical victory has induced but a few writers to barely mention the possibility of aerial law and that only the very recent accomplishments have drawn full attention to the subject. It is obvious one cannot be too careful with this sort of work. The projecting of detailed regulations for situations as yet unborn is sure to be not-worth-the-trouble, since one builds either on prophecies that will perhaps never be realised at all, or perhaps in an altered form; or one proposes rules regarding the few facts that are actually accomplished, thus building on an insufficient basis, overlooking all further development. In both cases one can be sure that the work will be obsolete before the time for application has arrived.

The reason why we begin by emphasizing this simple principle is because it has been somewhat overlooked by a most eminent author, Fauchille, who wrote an elaborate article on aerial law. At the Neuchâtel session of the International Law Institute, held in 1900, he was appointed chief reporter on the subject "the juridical position of aircraft", and he wrote a report and project of regulations going into the smallest details[2]), a conscientious work, but untimely. Feeling this probably himself, he proposed at the next session of the Institute (Brussels 1902) not to discuss the whole project, but only the ground problem: airfreedom or not. However, report and project

---

1) See for instance.
Bonfils, Manuel de droit intern. publ. 1908, p. 859.
Hall, A Treatise on International Law; 1904, p. 540.
Meili, Das Luftschiff im internen Recht und Völkerrecht 1908, p. 51.
Scholz, Drahtlose Telegraphie und Neutralität 1905, p. 23.
Mérignhac, Les lois et coutumes de la guerre sur terre 1903, p. 194 (note 4).
Wilhelm, De la situation juridique des aéronautes, J. I. P. 1891, p. 440.
2) Annuaire de l'Inst. de dr. intern. XIX p. 19.

awaiting a more favourable time of discussion. [1])

The great authority of both the writer and the Institute, render it desirable that it be known, the said project does not form a sound basis for earnest discussions. As an eminent writer like Fauchille will not, after so many years, bring any part of the old study unreviewed into discussion, it would be unnecessary to warn against it, were it not that the project as it is has been recommended with great stress by several authors. [2]) Yet one could have foretold immediately that the practical use of Fauchille's essay could not equal the amount of labor it must have cost, because of his neglecting the principle: make no rules before there is any necessity for them. For his work views the state of aeronautics of those days, which is a state of technical imperfection offering no opening for a general use and therefore involving no need for minute regulations.

To give an example: Fauchille thinks chiefly of uncontrollable balloons, mentioning the controllable ones only "en passant", just to say that for them there will be still less difficulty to keep to the rules than there is for the uncontrollabe ones.

The detailed regulations will be easily put aside as far as the situations prove to be different from what Fauchille expected them to be. The general principles he lays down in his work though, are more dangerous, since in contrast with the minute regulations which show their uselessness in their very words, the principles only could show such by their arguments, of which they form but the conclusions. For the great principles his basis, that viewed only what had been accomplished

---

1) In the annual report of 1908, p. 349 the question is still referred to as "Question to be studied".

2) Thus Meili, who admires it so much, that he adds the whole "project of regulations" as an appendix to his own writing: "Das Luftschiff im internen Recht und Völkerrecht".

T. Meyer. Enkele beschouwingen over luchtscheepvaart, oorlog en neutraliteit. Militair-rechtelijk Tijdschrift, Maart 1909, p. 453.

See also:

Bonnefoy, Le Code de l'air 1909, p. 205—228.

A. Mérignhac, Traité de dr. publ. intern. 1907, II, p. 398.

Scholz, Archiv für öffentl. Recht 1905, p. 600.

Rolland, La télégraphie saus fil et le droit des gens. R. D. I. P. 1906, p. 58.

Ch. Julliot, De la propriété du domaine aérien. 1909, p. 13.

law in the air we must think of a period in which aerial navigation is sure and frequent, and of situations on land accomodated to the new state of things; we must not think like Fauchille of undirigible balloons as the principal sort of air machines, of a police working only on and from the ground and able to control every ascent and every landing; of fortifications remaining for ever as open to spying aeronauts as they are nowadays.

Less attention to the details and more attention to the probable situation of the aerial world and to the principles of its law — and his eminent pen would surely have written a report, that would have been of the greatest use to the Institute and to international law at large. Probably too, this broader view would have led him to leave out some of his propositions that really seem unfit for realisation, for instance, the proposition to forbid in principle all aerial circulation under 1500 M. (about 4500 feet); or to establish a severe control so as to prevent aeronauts from taking with them in the air camera's with a lens for a greater distance than the regulations allow; or to take measures requiring every person who wants to take a flight to produce guarantees of the strictest integrity [1]!

Recent years have proved such a splendid success for aeronautics that really it seems justifiable for law to begin to take its share in the aerial labour. The chance of land and sea traffic being overshadowed in a very near future by overwhelming masses of airships and aeroplanes may not be very great, yet it is evident that the great technical difficulties are conquered and what remains to be done is comparatively speaking but childwork. When genius has accomplished the great step talent soon follows with the many little steps that are required to finish the work; the much greater frequency of talent than of genius being another guarantee that the way to perfection will not be very long. However, until one is a good deal surer of

1) Paul Fauchille. Le domaine aérien et le régime juridique des aérostats, 1901,

quent use will be made of the air. People prophecying that in a couple of years old and young will be flying are surely too enthusiastic, yet it does not seem saying too much when taking it for granted that we are indeed progressing rapidly on the right way to technical perfection. The great majority of scientists consider a regular use of the airway in a not too distant period possible. And the fact that in this state of imperfection one is all the same earnestly striving to get to the establishing of regular air lines, shows that technical progress is closely followed by practical application. Therefore the time has come for international law to meditate on the many vital questions aerial navigation is beginning already to bring to the fore, and to try to get to an international agreement as to the general principles that are to govern the law in the air.

It may seem a drawback that these general principles have to be argued before we can know exactly what aerial navigation will bring us. The main factor however to govern these principles must be the safety and the welfare of the existing states which is a most positive basis to be sure, and moreover demanding before long a settling of the main principles.

Besides, an international agreement concerning the principles has the great advantage of cutting off the possibility of conflict. In former times every state would have decided for itself which line it was to take; for instance, the one would proclaim absolute freedom of flight; another would demand formalities, the honouring of its flag; another again would close the airspace to every foreigner; conflicts would arise, wars would probably not fail to follow and only a long time afterwards would one search for the custom and come to an agreement as to which principle seemed te be most equal to all interests. Modern civilisation and modern law of nations seem more inclined to work the other way. The practice of recent times has brought to the fore the great advantage of international regulation where international interests are concerned. To guarantee this advantage to air traffic, an international interest by excellence, will be safely built, the states all working together or each state for itself, according to the character of the cases.

The craving of our generation for certainty in law and for peace through common deliberation certainly points to the way we have just referred to. We cannot, therefore, agree with those, who are of opinion that the settling of a principle question is not the work of a diplomatic conference with practical purposes. Meurer for instance thinks it wise only to found and regulate an international air traffic league, thus tacitly giving foreigners leave to fly freely through the space above all the lands concerned, without referring to the question of sovereignty [1]). He mentions as an example of this method the wireless telegraphic conference of 1906, that granted the Hertz waves free passage without saying a word as to whether this right is based on universal air freedom or whether it has to be considered as a concession of the sovereign states.

We should say, the example chosen is not a happy one. First of all, the method is not without danger, which is clearly shown by the fact that some authors come to the conclusion that the convention, saying [2]) the signatory powers promise to have their wireless telegraph stations organised in such a way as to hinder other stations as little as possible, sanctions thereby the principle of airfreedom. It is obvious that one can call the convention with as much reason a sanction of the sovereignty principle, if you imagine the powers' thoughts having gone this way, which seems quite rational too: We, sovereign states, have guaranteed free passage for international telegrams over our territory since many years. We need not repeat this for every new sort of telegraph, the new one sharing in the privilege as a matter of course, unless we pronounce a declaration to the contrary. So wireless telegraphy over our territory is granted by virtue of our sovereignty, but we need not say so.

---

1) Meurer, Luftschiffahrtsrecht 1909, p 19.
2) Art. 8.

did not discuss the fundamental question, air freedom or sovereignty, since this is of but small importance for the telegraphy problem. For as there is no wireless telegraphy without stations and as at that time the stations were supposed to be placed either on the land or on a ship, that is at any rate in places where the state is undisputed sovereign, states had a sufficient object for limitations and regulations in those stations; restricting rules for the stations being as well restrictions for all wireless telegraphy emerging from the stations. Against foreign stations placed on its territory or on its ships, the state is sufficiently armed by its undisputed authority, and as to the mere passing of the waves, this was not considered to endanger the safety or the sovereignty of the underlying territory to such a degree as to make discussion of the sovereignty principle necessary.

As to aerial navigation, however, one cannot proceed in the same way. In the first place, aeronauts can do without stations, so restricting rules for the stations do not necessarily affect all aerial navigation. Prohibiting foreigners to make use of the stations on the territory, does not imply that the land is safe against foreigners ascending and landing there. Moreover, an airship hovering over the territory endangers the safety of people and property below, and therewith the safety and may be the sovereignty of the state. At any rate, it is evident that a passing airship cannot be classed with a passing wireless telegram. In view of such air machines as are using foreign state territory for their landings and ascents, and in view of such as are merely passing over the territory, it is obviously insufficient to give but rules concerning the stations. What we need especially are rules for machines and people whilst in the air above sovereign territories. So in contradistinction to the settling of the wireless telegraphic questions, the sovereignty question is for the regulation of aerial navigation a most vital one.

Meurer rightly observes [1]) that the different theories in this matter all have more or less the same aim, wishing to har-

---

1) Meurer, l. c. p. 13.

exigences of international traffic. Yet again, we cannot agree with his conclusion that therefore the conflict regarding the fundamental question has lost its sharpness. The different theories may tend to about the same end, yet their consequences are not the same. The sovereignty theory grants the state in the air every possible right that sovereignty implies; in the freedom theory the state enjoys only such rights as common accord will grant. It may be true that several partisans of airfreedom like Meili and Fauchille are ready to admit the necessity of so many rights of the groundstate that the freedom is driven to the background, but not all authors claiming freedom are so loyal where the rights of the groundstate are concerned. Moreover, their loyalty cannot possibly foresee every situation where such rights may be desirable.

As long as it is left an open question as to whether freedom or sovereignty is the principle adopted by the different states, the inevitable consequence will be difference of opinion. In many cases one state perhaps will act as a sovereign, whereas another may not feel inclined to respect other states' full air sovereignty. Altogether, such a state of things will involve a meddling uncertainty, quite out of place in modern international law. Concerning a sphere of such great importance and embracing so many and such different interests, it seems to be of great importance to discuss and, if possible, agree as to which standpoint states will take towards aeronauts. Those states which consider themselves sovereign over the airspace will like to have their sovereignty recognised by the other powers. And if an agreement proves unattainable, it will be better anyhow for the governments as well as for aeronauts to know which position the different states take in this matter. Therefore the sovereignty question is not a mere theoretic problem, it is one of great practical interest. Forming the basis of many further considerations it ought to take a pominent place amongst them.

CHAPTER I.

JURIDICAL POSITION OF THE AIRSPACE.

In this chapter we intend to consider the question as to which is the position the airspace takes actually in the law of nations, and which position it is to take in future. Must this be the same everywhere though the underlying parts of the surface of the globe show much difference in their juridical conditions? Or must it follow these differences and are we to distinguish between the space over state territory and the space over the high seas just the same as we distinguish between state territory and the high seas? Is it sufficient perhaps to grant the groundstate some rights over the airspace or must we consider the state sovereign up to a certain height? Or is there no sovereignty in the air, is the space a "res nullius" abiding its conqueror or perhaps destined to remain a "res nullius" like the sea?

We see, there are many possibilities and each of them involving a great difference in consequences. It is worth while to pause a moment at the different opinions given upon the question and to make a close search for the best solution.

SECTION I. DIFFERENT SOLUTIONS.

§ 1. Opinion of authors.

For the last twenty years many writers upon international law, feeling the approach of the successful navigation of the air, take some slight notice of the new sphere and literature

state cannot be left without any authority over what happens just above its territory, and secondly, one shrinks from the idea that aerial navigation could be the object of narrow-minded restrictions. To bring these two ends together — the undeniable interest of the groundstate and sufficient freedom of intercourse for aerial navigation — proves to be the great difficulty and leads to the most different, and often strained solutions. To think that the innovation, the general favourite, one of whose greatest charms seems to be the sensation of absolute liberty, could be doomed to submission to unnecessary legal limitations, perhaps even to an actual closing of the air frontiers by an unfriendly or a timorous state, is to the admirers of airsport so unacceptable that in their zeal to prevent this evil they often take but little notice of the interest and the right of the separate state. In our opinion this fear is exaggerated and unnecessary, considering the great interest all nations take in international traffic in general and the improbability of their drawing the line at this new means of international intercourse, unless there might be very good reasons for it. Aeronautics once having reached a state of sufficiency to assure a safe and useful traffic no state will thoughtlessly throw up unnecessary hindrances.

The conclusions of the authors who have referred to the question are of a wonderful variety, which we cannot show better than in giving these solutions in two words, leaving the discussion of them to another paragraph.

We can divide these authors in two principal groups: those who defend the principle of air freedom and those who claim sovereignty for the groundstate. To the former group are to be reckoned in the first place those who are for freedom without any restriction and also those who, though starting from the freedom principle still grant the groundstate some limited authority, either to an unlimited height or to a certain height only, in analogy with the territorial sea. The second group too may be subdivided in three. We can class in it not only the authors who are partisans of sovereignty without restrictions authority, writers who, starting from the sovereignty principle yet make a restriction either in height or by way of a servitude of free passage.

———

A. Freedom Principle.

Zeppelin [1]). Since fences high in the air are not imaginable there can be no question of forbidding international airtraffic, which must be regulated bij treaties, in analogy with international maritime law.

———

1. Partisans of air freedom without restriction.

Wheaton. The sea is an element, which belongs to all men like the air. No nation then has the right to appropriate it.

Bluntschli. States have no sovereignty over the air, because men cannot keep it within boundaries.

Pradier-Fodéré. Agrees with Bluntschli. The air is by its nature not susceptible of belonging to state domain.

Stephan. Of course the air is free.

Nys. On earth we are to such a high degree victims to laws and regulations, let us take care by all means, not to spoil the air in the same way. Law must not be the enemy of progress.

———

2. Airfreedom, restricted by some special rights of the groundstate without these rights being bound in height, is claimed by:

Institute of International Law (14 contra 9). The air is free; states have in time of peace and in time of war only such rights as are necessary for their conservation.

Stranz. In principle the air is free, but restricted by some rights of the groundstate.

———

[1] For the titles of the references see Appendix A.

the use of all nations, under reservation of such rights as are needed by the underlying land for its conservation.

> 1909. Jan. The air is free as the well known rule of law says. Although this is not yet as sure as for the sea, we can see the principle grow under our eyes.
>
> Febr. Freedom for aeronauts, but full guarantee of conservation of the state and of its special interests (in analogy with German private law). No horizontal limit.
>
> April. Airfreedom for aeronauts but the groundstate must rule over the airspace above its territory, for it must be able to protect its far reaching interests against airships and flyingmachines.

———————

3. By far the greatest number of partisans of airfreedom see the best solution in the institution of a territorial atmosphere.

Despagnet. The air is free in principle, though the state must have certain rights, perhaps by analogy with the coast waters, though this cannot yet be said with certainty.

Fauchille. The air is free. The states have only such rights as are necessary for its conservation. Therefore all aerial navigation must be prohibited in principle up to 1500 M. (about 4500 feet).

Rolland. Follows Fauchille.

Bonnefoy. Follows Fauchille.

Mérignhac. Airfreedom, except the territorial atmosphere, the height of which must be fixed by convention, but not to high.

Oppenheim. The territorial atmosphere is not a special part of the territory of the state, but the state must be allowed to control it and to exercise jurisdiction in it up to a certain height.

Ferber. Free, except a territorial zone, if possible not higher than 500 M. (about 1500 feet).

1. Meyer. Free, except a territorial zone, as high as the state can maintain its authorithy directly from the territory.

Van Tets. Free, except a territorial zone.

B. Sovereignty principle.

1. The theory just mentioned — some rights for the groundstate to a limited height — is closely followed by the theory of full sovereignty up to a certain height.

Von Holtzendorff. To state territory we will have to reckon the airspace, for instance up to 1000 M. (about 3000 feet) from the highest points of the land.

Rivier. There is also an aerial domain. It is not yet necessary to fix its height; it will have to be done by analogy with the sea, that is as far as the range of a gun, here probably of a rifle.

Chrétien. Sovereignty, though not higher than the means of defense reach, placed on the land or waterdomain.

Pietri. Sovereignty as high as it can be carried into effect, that is determined by the range of artillery from the highest point of the land.

Hilty. Sovereignty as far as the sway of the state reaches, that is the same as regarding the sea, as far as artillery reaches — not fixed to a certain height.

Von Bar. Up to 50 à 60 M. (about 150 and 180 feet) full sovereignty. Quite high there is no chance of exercising any authority; concerning the zone lying between it is difficult to form an opinion as yet.

Von Liszt. 1902. State territory includes the airspace as far as state authority can be carried into effect, either by gun or by airmachine.

---

2. Again another solution recognises sovereignty to an unlimited altitude, but restricted by a servitude of free passage for aeronauts.

Grünwald 1907. We seem justified to consider the airspace an appurtenance of the groundstate though with some restriction in analogy with German private law. On no account may the state have the right to prohibit international airtraffic.

    1908. State territory comprises the airspace but the rights of the state may not be exercised further than is strictly necessary. Rules hindering international traffic may but be made if the state interests make them absolutely necessary

Meurer. Sovereignty with this restriction that aeronauts must have the right of free passage.

A. Meyer. The state has but limited sovereignty over the airspace, about the same as over the maritime belt.

   3. A last group of authors stand up for full sovereignty without any restriction either in height or by a servitude We hope to demonstrate that this solution alone is acceptable and that there is no reason why it should be marked as an impediment to the development of international airtraffic.

Von Liszt 1906. State territory includes the airspace above the land- and waterdomain.

Grünwald 1909. The airspace is part of the groundstate. However, in the same way as where landtraffic is concerned, the state cannot with impunity make rules prohibiting or unreasonably impeding aerial traffic, unless for reasons recognised by the law of nations.

Von Ullmann. State territory includes the airspace as high as one can penetrate with human means.

Collard. Full imperium to an unlimited height.

Gemma. Sovereignty to an unlimited height.

Solicitors' Journal. Probably full sovereignty will be required because of aeronauts endangering the underlying land.

Baldwin. Every independent nation must have the right to regulate the use of the air above its territory in such manner as best to promote the public interest.

must the state have authority in the air, but: how much authority and to what height? We have therefore not before us a pure repetition of the "mare liberum" and "mare clausum" of bygone centuries, for the important part of aerial navigation will take place in those lower regions where nearly all recognise the right of control of the groundstate and do not demand a state of liberty like the liberty of the open sea. With a single exception the so-called partisans of freedom of the air only want a solution that assures to them the freedom of passage as a right instead of as a concession. On some of the sovereignty partisans the wish to protect aeronauts against law has had a similar effect and makes them propose a servitude of free passage, since they too want to assure the freedom of traffic not by virtue of the state sovereignty but as an exception on that sovereignty, recognised by the law of nations. At first sight the difference between this sovereignty group and the greater part of those who claim airfreedom is not very great, the latter group proposing freedom but many rights for the groundstate, the former asking sovereignty, but free passage for aeronauts. The rather slight difference in the immediate result of these two theories has brought some authors to the conclusion that it does not much matter what the nature of these rights may be. This conclusion is not surprising as it is the almost unanimously accepted one concerning the position of the territorial waters. There, too, international navigation has the right of free passage, whilst the riparian state has several undoubted rights, though the basis of these rights is a point of great diversity of opinion. However, in using this analogy one forgets that the cases are widely different. Whereas for the coast waters the conclusion that the nature of the said rights are practically unimportant is readily accepted as there it sounds like an afterthought, because it concerns a situation that really is rather certain, we cannot say so as regards the airspace, as the use that will be made of the airspace and the rights this use must needs involve, are not at all certain as yet.

tical for the moment, even then the fundamental question would not have lost its practical importance, first, because of the safety of the state, sovereignty giving the safe feeling that any measure can be taken which the state thinks desirable though others may deem such a measure unnecessary, and secondly, because of its dignity. This is certainly better served if the sovereign state gives the assurance that it has no intention of hampering international airtraffic more than absolutely necessary, than by that other construction of rights which paints the sovereign state going home from an international conference that bestowed upon it the favour of some more or less defined rights.

Moreover, the aforesaid conclusion is based on the supposition that these two theories include every solution, our review shows that this is not the case and the proposition of the servitude is even extremely unfrequent.

The observation that the result of these two theories is for the moment almost similar has its value for all that, as it can show the free-air-men that the right they ask can go together quite as well with the sovereignty theory. Surely they will not unnecessarily cling to their principle, seeing that the safety and dignity of the sovereign state are better served by the sovereignty principle, seeing that international intercourse can flourish under the system of sovereignty and is likely to be promoted rather than hampered by the states and seeing that their principle of freedom which they do not need, is already reduced by themselves to little more than a hollow phrase by the great number of concessions they want to grant the groundstate. Although expressions such as "the air is free" give the impression of absolute freedom being asked, it is certainty of passage they want, not freedom like that of the high seas. As soon as they are convinced of the extreme improbability of aerial navigation being hampered — and the favourite position of international traffic in general and aerial navigation in particular cannot fail to convince them — they must feel satisfied and the nature of the rights of the groundstate need not be for them a cause of further dispute. For them the great

freedom of the open sea. The sweeping proclamations such as "the air is free" and the like, not only remind us of the sea, but they are nearly always the result of a comparison with the sea. Meili, for instance, says [1]: "As in the course of time "the freedom of the sea has been proclaimed, the freedom of "the air seems to be but a parallel of the same thought, "demanded by nature." Mérignhac goes still farther, taking the analogy with the sea as already generally accepted [2]:... "Authors have accepted the right and most ingenuous thought "of assimilating the air with the sea, and in consequence of "letting the air, considered to be absolutely free, share in the "benefit of the freedom of the open sea."

It is obvious they argue in this way: the sea cannot be state property; the sea is free, such is the principle recognised long since. Can we, of the twentieth century, behave like jurists of the middle ages, can we hesitate to proclaim this beautiful principle for the air as well as we did for the sea? Surely we cannot hesitate! The air must be free, open to any one; no one can be sovereign there! — Thus far they can safely go. However, as soon as they leave these generalities and pay some attention to the actual condition of the airspace and of the underlying land, nearly all writers think the analogy with the high seas unsatisfactory. The result is that they acknowledge the groundstate's interest in ruling over that part of the space, which is the most important part to aeronauts. And so they gradually come from their high principle of freedom to a discussion of the many rights the groundstate requires. Thereby the freedom such as the freedom of the open sea has disappeared.

Wheaton, Bluntschli and Pradier-Fodéré, though claiming airfreedom without mentioning any restriction, have obviously had only in mind the air as an element. They do not touch the question of the airspace, which is the only one of importance

---

1) Meili, Die Luftschiffahrt und das Recht. Die Zukunft 24 Apr. 1909, p. 121.
2) Mérignhac, La Conférence internationale de la Paix, 1900, p. 80.

different thing from the airfreedom viewed by the present dispute.

Zeppelin, referring to the question in a technical lecture, seems to allude to a state like that of the open sea, though, of course, he does not go farther into the juridical question. Stephan proposes the freedom of the air, in a non juridical work, and without any argumentation.

The only writer one can call an actual supporter of the freedom principle is Nys. Sighing over the great number of laws and regulations spoiling man's freedom on earth, he fervently hopes that up in the air fate will be milder and lock out all laws. We are afraid indeed, humanity is not yet ripe for this desired state of freedom from law.

All others of the freedom group recognise that a given portion of the airspace is indeed of far greater interest to the underlying land than to all other points of the globe. The necessity of the groundstate having authority in the air is obvious and the sea analogy having already once been adopted, suggests, as a matter of course, the institution of an aerial belt. Most of them though, take care to leave the difficult point, namely the settling of the height of this belt, to the wisdom of a conference [1]). The part of the airspace this solution leaves free cannot, however, be of much importance to aeronauts . At least, we can think of no good reason why the proposed aerial belt should be of less extent than the maritime belt, the airspace, as has been often said, being, by its position above the land, nearer to the country than the sea that is only at its sides. At any rate, the opinion that an aerial belt should be of less importance to the land than its coast waters are, is not supported by a single writer and indeed could not well be maintained. Therefore, it seems to be extremely improbable that the limit of an aerial belt should be laid lower than three miles at least, being the generally adopted breadth of the territorial waters. Now three miles amply include the sphere where aerial

1) See, for instance, Mérignhac. Traité de droit public international 1907 II p. 406, where he says that the territorial atmosphere must be high enough to guarantee the

ding to this solution, the condition will be thus: freedom for the higher regions of which very little use will be made, and the lower part — i. e. the important part — on about the same conditions as the coast waters. Whosoever is content with this, cannot be said in earnest to proclaim in favour of aerial navigation a state of freedom such as the freedom of the open sea.

Fauchille, in proposing to close the zone under 1500 M. (about 4500 feet) in principle to all aerial navigation, almost excludes airtraffic thereby, though he is the first to proclaim the air free! He, too, only demands freedom for the less important higher regions. No more is Meili for freedom in reality. Though saying that the air must be free "like the sea," he comes all the same more and more to the conviction that the underlying land has such a very special interest in all goings-on in the air, that the state must be allowed to rule there. He even suggests a solution by analogy with German private law, which means that he actually goes over to the sovereignty principle. For German private law gives in unmistakable terms the proprietor of the soil a right over the whole airspace covering the soil, though restricted by a duty of tolerance regarding such doings as are of no interest to him. An analogous solution for the air question implies a state that is rather the reverse of the freedom of the open sea than its image.

Reviewing these solutions of the supporters of the freedom principle has taught us that with a single exception they do not propose, in reality, a state like that of the high seas for the airspace. Their solutions are by no means a better guarantee than is sovereignty for that freedom of intercourse they pretend to bring with so much certainty.

Another comparison with the maritime belt we find again in the solutions of those who uphold the sovereignty principle, but do not want to grant that sovereignty to an unlimited height and suggest taking the old rule "range of artillery" for measuring its altitude. Rivier adds that probably the rifle alone can be used to determine this. We fail to see the

prophecy would not have been too rash that supposed artillery construction to keep pace with new inventions and new wants. And indeed Krupp has already constructed a special gun, capable of shooting nearly vertically 7400 M. (about 22200 feet) [1]) and is sure to increase this height in course of time.

The little bit of free air this theory is good enough to grant is of no account for aerial navigation — and for the important part it claims full sovereignty.

Ullmann's limit: as far as one can penetrate by human means, reaches as far as aerial navigation goes and, therefore, it can be placed practically on a line with full sovereignty.

We see all these writers, though pretending to leave part of the airspace free, again do not guarantee the freedom of intercourse any better than does the full sovereignty theory.

Besides these restrictions as to the height of the state sovereignty, we find the proposed restriction by servitude. Again we fail to see the necessity of establishing this servitude of free passage. What these writers want, like those who pretend to claim airfreedom, is nothing more than certainty of traffic, which can be sufficiently attained, however, without proclaiming the air free, or establishing a servitude of free passage, without attacking the state interest and dignity, which demand sovereignty in the air as well as on the land.

Thus, not one of the proposed restrictions seems justified, none of the objections against full sovereignty valid. Certainty of international traffic can go quite well together with full sovereignty, the best proof of this contention being international landtraffic. Moreover, the states' self-interest obliges them not to be behindhand in the world's traffic, and is therefore the best guarantee for their not hampering aerial traffic more than necessary.

To satisfy those who might consider this guarantee insufficient, a treaty could perhaps be signed, containing the states' promise to treat foreign and national aeronauts alike.

---

dignity of the state is left intact, and aerial navigation will not be hampered in its development.

SECTION II. COMPARISONS.

As we have said before, the comparison of sea and air has played its part in the proposed solutions concerning the principles of aerial law. Though the analogy is rejected by several authors, these often go too far in the opposite direction, since the general disposition and nature, the wide expanse, the continual changing of both sea and air certainly justify a comparison to some extent. For why do we compare? To find cases where existing rules can be applied, to lighten the work of lawmakers. And in the air there will certainly be cases where maritime rules apply. So, starting from the absolute assertion that analogy with the sea is wholly out of court, in similar cases one will either get involuntarily to similar rules, or afterwards, when the conformity of the cases becomes obvious, one will review the regulations; at any rate, the way of analogy, where it is possible, is the shorter way.

It is not surprising, however, that the critics of the comparison theory exaggerate a little and reject the whole comparison, since the observing of some points of conformity has led already to an example of blind following of maritime rules, namely, to the proclaiming of airfreedom as a consequence of the analogy with the sea.

Both theories go too far. The mistake is in saying too much as to there being no place whatever for analogy, but absolute analogy is quite as objectionable. An impartial comparison will show, there are points of conformity and points of difference, this will lead to other comparisons and to the conclusion that there are also many points and situations in the aerial future which are original and want original rules. The sorting of these analogous and original characteristics is a first condition to the

for the new field of law.

---

§ 1. Comparison with the open sea.

Sea and air considered as elements, apart from any relation to the land, are so much alike that it is but natural so many authors have taken this comparison as the starting-point of their deliberations.

The sea, one says, is invincible, not capable of being kept within human frontiers, because of its nature — this is also the case with the air.

The sea is incapable of bearing any fixed boundary marks or fixed marks of occupation — so is the air.

Therefore no sovereignty can be exercised over the sea and therefore none over the air either. Is this consequence justified? We think not.

First of all, in these arguments the old error — the error of considering the air as the object of discussion instead of the air-space, which after repeated criticism, again and again turns up — is obvious. Sovereignty wants a sphere, a domain, where it can be exercised. In theory it is of no account what there may be in that sphere; and in practice? Is the fact that it is filled with a moving element, where fixed marks cannot well be magined, enough to make sovereignty there practically impossible? We think not. We think rather this conclusion has again its origin in a too great wish for analogy. Because on land the signs of sovereignty — buildings and boundary marks — can have a fixity, which in sea and air is out of the question, is sovereignty there quite unacceptable? Is it really as inseparable as that of the fixity of these marks? May we really call a deciding argument against the possibility of sovereignty the fact, that neither a ship nor an air machine can leave any sign on the spot they have left? [1] Does it not sound more rational to judge every sphere after its own nature? Difference in substance can ask for difference in application of the sovereignty principle. This principle

---

1) Fauchille. l. c.. p. 19.

to rule without fixed boundary marks, he is nevertheless sovereign. There is no reason why one should make it a condition that sea and airfrontiers must be established in a way such as to make it possible to respect them literally to an inch, which, of course, is only possible on land.

It is curious that one is so ready to exclude the possibility of sea and airfrontiers, wholly forgetting that history as well as modern practice recognise their possibility, at least of borders in the water. For long years sovereignty over parts of the high seas has been known and recognised [1]), nor can it be denied that authority over parts of seas and rivers nowadays exist without any fixed boundary marks. The borders of ports and gulfs and of the territorial waters; the so-called Thalweg, the frontier that follows the middle of the river separating two countries, are an example of water frontiers, lacking the fixedness of frontiers on land. They are therefore, perhaps, more apt to be the cause of international conflict, but neither their existence nor the possibility of such existence is disputed by any one. For the same reason air frontiers are sure to give rise to practical difficulties, they have in fact already done so at the German-Russian frontier (Aug. 1909) where it is said Russians fired at the balloon Tschudi, as it was above German soil. However, the impossibility of placing in the air signs as settled as those on land can be no more an obstacle to air-sovereignty than it is to water-sovereignty.

The freedom of the open sea is nevertheless considered a desirable institution. One thinks the interest of all nations' international traffic together with no nation's obvious interest in having special authority over a far-off part of the sea, a ground sufficient for its existence. In other words, the relation between the open sea and the land makes such freedom desirable and compatible with the existence and the interests of all nations. And in this relation with the land, the basis of the freedom of the high seas, we find the main point of difference between sea and air. It is obvious that a real difference in this rela-

1) Hall, A Treatise on International Law 1904, p. 141.

possibly determine on declaring the air free for other reasons, but the proposed analogy, proclaiming the air free *because* the sea is free, is decidedly wrong.

The relation between the airspace and the underlying sovereign territory is indeed widely different from the relation between sea and land. First, sea traffic established the connection between countries that could not traffic with each other in any other way, airtraffic over sovereign territory will only be an addition to the intercourse by land. Secondly, no land seems predisposed to be sovereign over a particular part of the open sea, whereas for a given part of the airspace the underlying land undoubtedly is. The sea being "res nullius" does not hurt the rights of any state, is of no direct importance to any territory. The farther we are off in a horizontal direction, the less direct utility and the less direct danger the land may expect from us. So the institution of the maritime belt, placing the free sea at a considerable distance from the land, really means a measure of safety for that land. What happens outside the maritime belt is not often likely to re-act upon the land.

As regards the space above the land, however, all this is quite different. Indeed "above the land" is a different thing from "at the side of the land"; the state interest in what happens above the territory does not stop at any stated height, a great distance in a vertical direction by no means implies proportionally less danger for the underlying land, a fall from a higher point producing even an increased rapidity in falling. The institution, for instance, of a maritime belt of such breadth as is within effective range of the shore batteries is sufficient to protect the land against artillery placed outside the belt, the range of artillery being the same in either sense in a horizontal direction. Such reciprocity, however, would absolutely fail to exist where an aerial belt is concerned, the institution of which never can protect the land against projectiles from airships flying higher than the belt's border.

And thirdly, the first conditions of human life and, therefore, of human traffic do not diminish the farther one is off the

navigation, whereas such division of the airspace would be of no such consequence, proclaiming free only the unimportant highest zones.

The comparison with the open sea only justifies analogous application of such regulations where the relation with the land is not concerned; for instance, for the aforesaid question of the frontiers and especially for many cases of practical navigation rules, which are sure to apply to cases of aerial navigation.

---

§ 2. Comparison with the maritime belt.

Similarity between the airspace and the maritime belt exists so far as in both cases there is the riparian country with a very special interest, whereas for the not riparian countries the only thing that matters is surety of internatial traffic. In both cases there is not a shadow of a doubt as to which country is to have authority, if any.

Secondly, both airspace and territorial waters are but secondary parts of state territory, never the principal.

The great difference, though, lies in the fact that, where the maritime belt is not strictly necessary for the existence of the state, the airspace is. The right of control and of jurisdiction over the territorial waters is, to be sure, highly important for the safety of the state, the right of fishery and of cabotage interesting for its wealth, but these rights cannot be called necessary for its existence. For instance, where the sea gets too narrow for two maritime belts of normal breadth, both riparian states have a belt of less extent, but without any decrease of sovereignty. And even were all the rights of the state to cease on the line that separates the sea from the land, its sovereignty would be as intact as ever, the sea frontiers being in such a case only in the same condition as the land frontiers. Concerning the airspace, circumstances are indeed widely different again. As human beings cannot live in a plane, the state, having to deal with living people, is obliged to have a domain of three dimensions. And man preferring to live not under

the necessary third dimension extend above the surface too.
Placing the airfrontiers just where the land ceases would therefore make the land worthless, the existence of the state practically impossible. Sovereignty over a piece of land neccessarily implies full sovereignty over the lower zones of the space above it; this is too obvious for contradiction, though often forgotten.

The only conclusion to be drawn from this comparison can be that the space above the land is nearer in interest to the groundstate than the part of the sea that is next to the land, and that, consequently, the state has more interest in excluding other states from having rights over its airspace than it has in excluding them as regards the territorial waters. There is no reason, anyhow, to claim the right of free passage for aeronauts by analogy of the right of free passage through the territorial waters.

---

§ 3. Comparison with the land.

Although air-and land-domain are different in character, the land always being the principal part, the starting-point of state territory, and the airspace only figuring as a supplement, making the exercise of sovereignty on the land possible, yet there is much likeness between the two. Both land and airspace are essential for the existence of the state [1]), and both are important to other countries as an international highway. As landtraffic has reached a high degree of international development without there ever having been question about a servitude, nor about loss or decrease of sovereignty, the assertion that one of these measures should be necessary for the development of international airtraffic, becomes worthless.

---

§ 4. Comparison with international rivers.

Comparing the airspace with international rivers we find this

---

1) Compare § 2.

sea and thereby other countries.

International rivers, however, are for navigation a generally indispensable connection with the sea, the lower river being in most cases not only the shortest but also the only way to the open sea. As regards the airspace, a similar necessity of passage, of a way out to the sea, could only be claimed by a country not having any sea frontier. Such countries, however, being extremely rare, the case would seem more apt for regulation by special treaty between the countries concerned, and is by no means fit to be the basis of a general principle. Countries bordering on the sea can reach all other countries equally bordering on the sea, that is almost all other countries, through the airspace over the open sea. Although the concession of passing over foreign countries may be of great importance, there is no question here of necessity, of a way out, so we see no reason why one should place the airspace under an analogous regime as that of the international rivers.

---

§ 5. Comparison with ports, gulfs etc.

The ports and gulfs — as far as they are not part of the open sea — are generally considered to be part of the state territory; they are moreover of eminent importance for international navigation.

This leads to the same conclusion as the comparison with the land domain. As the ports and gulfs stand under full state sovereignty and international traffic is flourishing all the same, it is evident that air sovereignty alone need not be an obstacle for the development of international airtraffic.

---

§ 6. Conclusion.

Resuming the results of these comparisons, we see that they can by no means be called favourable for the airfreedom or for the servitude of free passage. We saw that the high seas and the airspace are so little alike in relation to the land, that there may be no question of analogous adoption of the freedom

deration for analogy because of the fundamental difference-authority in the air being a necessity for the groundstate, rights over the maritime belt, on the contrary, not more than a privilege for the riparian state. Then we saw, there is neither any reason why one should take the regime of the international rivers as an example for the airspace. But what above all stands out clearly after these comparisons is the fact, that it is most unjust to call sovereignty an impediment for the development of international traffic. If aerial intercourse of some importance proves to be practically possible, state sovereignty, though it may touch the utter limit of the atmosphere, need not be, nor is it probable to be, an obstacle for such development.

***

SECTION III. RELATION BETWEEN THE LAND AND THE SPACE ABOVE IT.

A. The groundstate's right to recognition of its air-sovereignty.

We have mentioned as one of the characterictics of the airspace that it is an essential part of the state territory and therefore must be as fully submitted to the state sovereignty as the land. We have not yet discussed the point, however, as to whether it is sufficient to recognise sovereignty for the lower part only of the airspace or whether this authority must be unlimited in height. For, arguing that sovereignty need not be an obstacle for the development of international airtraffic is not identical with showing that sovereignty unlimited in height is the best solution. Considering the relation of the airspace with the land and considering the interpretation science and practice have given of that relation, as far as they had the occasion to give their opinion, we got the conviction that it is the best one, and we hope to prove so in the following pages.

***

§ 1. Objections against a horizontal limit.

As we have said before, sovereignty over a piece of land is worth

also over everything between these buildings, whether touching the ground or not touching it. No state, indeed, is likely to consider an aeroplane, soaring just above the soil along buildings that reach to the sky, to be moving outside its sphere of sovereignty. Or, to give a less modern example: a couple of workmen who are working on a high tower and quarrelling tumble down, and in the air wound or kill each other, may be sure to find a policeman and a judge, who consider them to have committed the deed within the sphere of their jurisdiction. This being so, condemns the theory that says: sovereignty reaches as high as the buildings do. For then this formula cannot mean only the space filled by buildings, but must imply also the space between, and this extension makes the standard lose its usefulness, the buildings being too different in height and in many cases being placed at a great distance from each other or existing not at all. As regards houses that stand apart one would perhaps consider every house decisive for the space around it; but then, how far around? And what is to be the standard for lonely places where there are no buildings? Then, as regards the space between two houses of different height standing near to each other, the highest one would probably be taken for measure; but then again, how far around is that higher house to be decisive? Only for the nearest houses? For a whole town? a whole country? Would one high tower suffice to give a land as high a frontier in the air? Or perhaps for the sake of equality, are we to take for universal measure the highest monument on earth [1]), which is, at the present time, the Eiffel Tower, about 900 feet high, and but recently made still higher by an installation for wireless telegraphy? Then every higher monument would increase the sphere of sovereignty of all states, and the disappearance of this all-important monument would mean a lowering of sovereignty all over the globe! We see, great certainty is not to be expected from this method of measuring sovereignty.

---

1) Compare Fauchille, l. c., p. 7.

soil, there is no reason to exclude the captive balloon from this honour. The captive balloon is a construction which, though not being as steady as the Eiffel tower, is unanimously considered to be a dependance of the soil and thus standing under the full sovereignty of the groundstate. Though generally stationed at a height of 1000—2000 feet, it sometimes does reach 3600 feet. Then, one could, by maintaining a captive balloon high in the air, keep the world's sovereignty for the time being much higher, though still more uncertain, than by the Eiffel tower measuring. This necessary consequence of accepting the captive balloon as a measure clearly shows that the theory which grants sovereignty as high as the buildings go, offers a measure which is far too uncertain to be acceptable.

Still less certainty is to be found in the most objectionable theory: sovereignty as high as man can see, a theory mentioned and criticised by Fauchille [1]). This theory is another proof of the bad working of a forced analogy with the sea. The measure has been proposed to fix the extent of the maritime belt and as such, though rather vague, it is based on thought, for there certainly is a limit beyond which from the shore the best eyes, and were they a thousand times better than human eyes, cannot see anything of the round globe. In a vertical line, on the contrary, any such natural horizon failing, the theory loses its thought and becomes impracticable, for the only way to apply it there would be first to fix the size of the object that has to been seen, the degree of details one must distinguish etc. etc.

"Sovereignty as high as artillery, placed on the territory, reaches," gives pratically a good height already, which is sure to be increased still more, as one may safely suggest the construction of guns will further improve in this direction. Theoretically, however, this measure is not much better than the others, as again it is not founded on a sound basis. Why should one make the condition that the artillery must be placed on

1) Fauchille, l. c., p. 16.

exercising authority will prove to be by means of airships.
If so, the construction of high reaching guns will not be necessary to enforce sovereignty, but only to measure and obtain it! As a measure of safety this theory is, moreover, of no consequence, there being no correspondence whatever between the range of a shot upwards and downwards.

Besides the amount of uncertainty, there is another great objection against all these theories. Were the surface of the earth smooth and even, the airfrontier would be at the same height up in the air all over the globe, smooth and even also. The earth's surface, however, being far from smooth, we are faced with the alternative, must the limit of sovereignty be measured from some certain, recognised, universal mark, or must it follow all the ups and downs of the soil?

A strong argument against the first solution would be that one would be obliged tc place the limit at a very great height to make sure that the highest parts of the soil do not tower above the sphere of sovereignty. This solution is, moreover, unjust towards high lands, these getting the limit of their authority much nearer their territory than low lands do.

The second solution, making the airfrontier follow every unevenness of the soil, seems to be much more reasonable. But there are sound objections also against this one. For assuming such a limit of the authority in the air, means taking a measure which will be a great nuisance for every one who has to reckon with it, a measure, moreover, that is very unjust towards low lands, as the atmosphere certainly does not follow all the ups and downs. The air being much thinner on the top of a high mountain than at is base, the addition of a sphere of sovereignty of the same extent above high lands and above low lands, will put these two categories of countries in a different position towards aerial navigation. For the high land an airdomain of considerably little height will be sufficient to bring almost all aerial traffic below its air boundary. For the low land on the contrary an airdomain of the same height will be of little value, aerial navigation being able to remain without much difficulty beyond the airborders of such a state. At any rate, aeronauts

the zone they find above the airdomain of high lands. Accordingly it will be much easier to keep or get out of the way of the authority of the low land than of the high land.

Both solutions are unequal and unsatisfactory. The objections against the horizontal limit, it seems to us, are unable to be removed.

---

§ 2. Sovereignty, unrestricted in height.

One of the reasons, perhaps the reason, why many authors come to a restriction in height, seems to be that, when considering the sovereignty question, they start from a false thought. They do not sufficiently keep in view the right and the interest of the groundstate, they consider the airspace as a domain which has still to be taken possession of. In reality there is no question here of establishing new sovereignty but of recognising sovereignty that exists, as we will see later on.

That sovereignty includes the very lowest part of the airspace, is a generally acknowledged fact. However, when trying to realise what sovereign states mean by this very lowest part, one soon comes to the conviction, they never, when regulating their interests, have thought for a moment of the possibility of their not being competent to give rules reaching as high as they thought necessary. Although, of course, in most cases making laws only for the space that is quite near to the soil, they never hesitated, when circumstances made it desirable, to extend their authority quite as well to higher regions.

The living in high houses already involves an exercise of sovereignty in higher regions than where one lives in very low houses. If people were going to live in high towers, no state, to be sure, would scrupulously consider whether its sovereignty reaches to the space around the top of those towers. The sphere of its silently recognised sovereignty over the airspace rises according as the houses or other interests reach higher. As long as this rising is gradual and especially as long as no opposite interest makes its appearence, no one objects. It is the suddenness of

combined with the wish to protect aerial navigation against the slightest impediments, that makes many a writer hesitate to recognise that leap in the air of the exercise of state sovereignty. They overlook the fact that only the exercise of sovereignty enters into an almost new domain, not sovereignty itself. Houses do give the limit beneath which sovereignty has, until recently, for the greater part been exercised, but not because these buildings are one with the soil, but because people are wont to use houses standing on the ground and vehicles touching the same, in short, because by far the greater part of human life — and thus of state interests — is very close to the earth as yet. If its interests lie in higher regions, state sovereignty makes itself felt there too, such is the practice which all nations silently recognise.

And it is but natural that the state should consider its authority to reach as high as it thinks fit, because of the state needing the airspace for its existence, and because of everything in the air being a possible danger to the underlying land. We hope to show that the states never have hesitated to regulate, when necessary, interests disclosing themselves in spheres beyond houses and towers.

----

§ 3. Opinion of Law, Literature and Jurisprudence.

As a matter of course, there have not been many cases in which the states could have shown their sovereignty in higher regions; yet enough to be a practical affirmation of our theoretical assertion. The inquiry we made on this subject, has strengthened our conviction. Wherever we inquired, in national or in foreign law, we always found some rules comprising, more or less clearly, interests in higher spheres, and we found that the opinion of lawyers, writers and judges almost unanimously sustain our theory. We are confident the summary of the result of this inquiry will give others the same conviction, that the sovereign state has never felt bound to limit itself to any height.

First of all, we want to refer to the rules of civil law concerning the extent of land-property. The state cannot give the landowner a right of property or of use over the airspace above his land, if that airspace is not submitted to its sovereignty. Consequently, by giving such a right to the landowner, the state says that it considers itself sovereign over the airspace. Now almost every one is of opinion that the landowner has a legal right over the space above his land.

In almost every country private law concerning the extent of land-property is ruled by the old adage "Cujus est solum ejus est usque ad coelum", which rule the Code Napoléon, the example of so many countries' law, contains in these words (art. 552): "la propriété du sol comprend la propriété du dessus et du dessous" (the property of the soil includes the property of what is over and under it). Portalis recommends this rule in the memorial to the Code project as a necessity, saying [1]): "One will understand that property would not be perfect.... if he (the landowner) were not master of the whole space his domain encloses". So, though the words of the Code could perhaps justify a narrow interpretation, the Portalis explanation shows clearly in which direction the meaning of the Code makers lies, namely, to extend the landowner's right not only to what is one with the soil, but to the whole space covering the land.

With a rare exception all writers maintain this opinion and recognise the landowner's right over the airspace as over an appurtenance of the land. We refer to: [2]) Théophile Huc, Baudry- Lacantinerie, Aubry et Rau, Dalloz, Laurentie, Passion, Cirier, Julliot. Of another opinion are Naquet, who says property of the airspace only exists as far as the space is really used by what has been built or planted on the soil, and Planiol, who considers the property above the land a question that can only be treated under the head accretion and who consequently thinks the rule of art. 552 C. N. is only referring to objects connected with the soil.

We find again the maxim "Cujus est solum ejus est usque

---

1) Code civil suivi de l'Exposé des Motifs. 1820, IV, p. 38.

in the law of many a country: in the codes of Germany, Switzerland, Italy, the Netherlands, Belgium, Spain, Portugal, Austria, Japan, Turkey, in the old law of Germany — which was in vogue until its recently accepted code —, in several of the old codes of the Swiss Cantons, in the unwritten law of England and America and in the project of a Code of Hungary [1]).

All these provisions have either the redaction of the French Code, or they express — with the exception only of the Dutch one — the principle on which they are founded still more distinctly than the Code does. The law of Germany, Switzerland, Austria, Hungary, Italy, Portugal, and that of several Swiss Cantons, speak of a right over the airspace instead of the somewhat vague expression: "propriété du dessus". As regards these plain expressions there can be no doubt but that they sustain our opinion. Nor may the others be interpreted differently, for they are either based on the Code or, having independently from the Code come to a like definition, they are founded like the Code on the old principle "Cujus est solum ejus est usque ad coelum."

Here again our opinion finds much support in literature. See for instance [2]): Werenberg, Jehring, Hesse, Dernburg, Windscheid, Meili, Planta, Huber, Wieland, Schey, Krainz, Thomas Brett, Blackstone, Stephen, Pollock, Baden-Powell, Law Journal, Solicitors' Journal, Mc. Clean, Reeves, Coke, Kent, Words and Phrases; they are all of them of opinion that the landowner has a legal right over the airspace covering his land. They only differ as to the nature of the said right, some calling it a proprietor's right, others a right of use, whereas others again only recognise a right of use if, and as far as such use is necessary for the use of the land. So there is no doubt as to the existence of a legal right over the airspace, there is only difference of opinion as to the nature and the extent of the right. Now the nature of this right is of no consequence for our research after manifestations of sovereignty in higher regions, as the granting of a right of use is as well a deed of sovereignty as the granting of a right of property. So we

---

1) See Appendix B. 1.

and such as call it a right of use, both interpretations being an affirmation of our view that most states have, by virtue of their sovereignty, established a right reaching high into the air.

Neither may the restriction made by some writers, that the right reaches no higher than is strictly necessary for the use of the land or the interest of the landowner, be referred to as if not following our view. For, generally, this restriction does not mean to limit the right in height, it just means to give a solution like the sensible definition of the German Code, which says that the landowner's right extends up to an unlimited height, but that all the same he is not entitled to prohibit such doings as are of no importance to him. So the writers who give an interpretation in this sense equally affirm our view. And even if the said restriction should mean to give only a right of limited height, it is clear that the height of this limit is fixed by the supposed extent of the landowner's interest. So even then the state has manifested its sovereignty as high as it thought necessary.

The Dutch Code has a definition which, though meant to be a literal translation of the French Code, is rather equivocal. Art. 626 says that land-property includes the property of anything that is on the land. Some very few writers think that this expression only refers to objects connected with the soil. See Land and Opzoomer [1]). By far the greater number of authors, however, prefer the interpretation that the expression "on the land" refers to the airspace. We name: Asser, Scholten, Diephuis, Fockema Andreæ, Levy, Cohen Tervaert, Modderman, Jacobson [2]). And really there is not much reason to take the expression too literally. For according to the French text of the Netherland Code of 1830 [3]) and according to a government declaration given during the discussions [4]) the article is meant to say exactly the same as art. 552 C. N. Moreover, we find in

1) See Appendix B. 2.
2) See Appendix B. 2.
3) Art. 672.
4) J. C. Voorduin. Geschiedenis en beginselen der Nederlandsche Wetboeken 1838

the report of these discussions the expression "above the ground" [1]), which no one has objected to, though these words certainly exclude all necessity of connection with the soil.

To give an example of the above principle, authors usually refer to the legal rules concerning adjoining landowners, rules that consider overhanging buildings and overhanging trees as a trespass on the right of the neighbour [2]).

B. Laws Concerning Aerial Electric Wires.

A more recent case of applying the principle has been caused by the overground electric wires. The right to stretch wires over another's land has often been objected to with the principle "Cujus est solum ejus est usque ad coelum". Such objections have led in most countries to laws positively establishing the required right and thereby recognising the necessity of this right having a legal basis, because it is a restriction of the landowner's right. Instances of such legal provisions are to be found in the following laws [3]):

The Netherlands. Law to regulate communication by means of electro-magnetic telegraphs, 7th March 1852. Off. Gaz. 48, art. 4.

Law concerning the construction, exploitation and use of telegraphs and telephones, 11th Jan. 1904, Off. Gaz. 7, art. 7.

France. Loi sur les distributions d'énergie, 15 juin 1906, art. 12.

England. Telegraph Act 1863 (26 & 27 Vict. Cap. 112) S. 21.

Germany. Telegraphenwege-Gesetz. 1899. § 12.

United States of America. State of New-York. Transportation Corporation Law, art. VIII.

Louisana. Act n° 124, 1880. Ann. de législ. étrang. X p. 689.

---

1) J. J. F. Noordziek. Geschiedenis der beraadslagingen gevoerd in de Tweede Kamer der Staten-Generaal over het ontwerp van Burgerlijk Wetboek. 1823—24, p. 67.

2) See for instance: Art. 714 and 695 Dutch Code; Code Nap. art. 673 and 678; B. G. B. §§ 910 and 912; Schweiz. Z. G. B. art. 674; C. c. italien art. 582 and 587;

Italy. Legge sui telefoni 7 apr. 1892, art. 5.

Testo unico della legge sui telefoni. Gazz. uff. 3 Maggio 1903, art. 4.

Switzerland. Loi fédérale concernant l'établissement de lignes télégraphiques et téléphoniques, 26 juin 1889 F. féd. III p. 897. art. 2.

Belgium. Loi qui ouvre un crédit au département des travaux publics pour pourvoir àl'achèvement des lignes télégraphiques. 14 avr. 1852. Mon. du 20 avr. 1852. art. 4.

Loi du 23 mai 1876 autorisant des concessions de télégraphie locale. Mon. du 28 mai 1876. art. 5.

Loi concernant l'établissement et l'exploitation de réseaux téléphoniques, 11 juin 1883. Mon. du 12 juin 1883. art. 4.

Such discussions of these laws as we have been able to consult (Holland, France, Germany, Belgium) showed us clearly that the makers considered the stretching of wires over another's property unlawful unless legally admitted. We even found the opinion that the proposed restriction of the landowner's right was a serious one, apt to reduce the value of the land, as the wires would probably be a great nuisance to the proprietor of the land [1]). In most cases, however, the restriction was considered to be a very light one indeed, and has been enacted without difficulty. Some few laws even went farther. Considering the restriction to be of but the slightest importance they leave it out altogether. So for instance the first German Telegraph Act [2]), during the discussions of which act the commissioner of the federal government positively said [3]) that the act meant to contain only what was strictly necessary and leaves to a later act several points that could wait, amongst which he names the right to stretch wires over the houses. Again, we find the positive restriction failing in the French Telegraph and Telephone Act of 1885 [4]), because the great urgency of the

---

1) See for instance the Dutch "Handelingen 2e Kamer" 1884—1885, p. 1048.
2) Gesetz über das Telegraphenwesen des Deutschen Reichs. 6 April 1892.
3) Verhandlungen des Reichstages 1890—1891. p. 1962.
4) Loi relative à l'établissement, à l'entretien et au fonctionnement des lignes

and houses to allow the placing of the wires, made it undesirable and unnecessary to elaborate this part of the act [1]). The English lawmaker thinks more of the restriction and requires for the right to stretch overhead wires the permission of the owner, lessee and occupier of the land or building.

C. Game Laws.

Hunting and the protection of birds are subjects that undoubtedly have led to legal provisions in the air, i. e. to manifestations of sovereignty in higher regions.

That laws, wherever they deal with birds, should refer only to birds touching the ground, is too improbable a suggestion to be acceptable. Many provisions would lose their value by such a narrow interpretation, and many rules, moreover, positively contradict it. The Dutch Game law (art. 29) for instance, promises renumeration for the killing of noxious birds on one's own ground and amongst them it names high-flying birds such as the eagle, the hawk, the falcon, etc. Surely there would not be much chance of a fairly good success, if the interpretation were right, that only such eagles and hawks are meant as touch the soil when being shot at. The same act says in art. 21 that nets to catch some special birds may not be placed lower than a certain height. Can these nets refer to birds touching the soil?

There is another part of game law where the necessity of considering the law to be meant equally for birds when flying comes still stronger to the fore. All civilized nations distinguish between shooting season and close season, and nearly all have birds' protection acts. In both cases law forbidding the killing of birds must be accepted in the broadest possible sense. To except all flying birds would make the prohibition almost valueless.

The like might be said concerning the killing of noxious birds. In several countries the permission to do so is given

---

1) Rapport fait au nom de la Commission par M. Esnault, journ. off. août 1885

the killing is prohibited. But then again there would not be much sense in this prohibition if it were confined to birds touching the soil.

Then also the rule, practised by most countries, that forbids hunting on ground where one has no legal right to do so, would miss a good deal of its effect if flying birds were excepted. Considering on the contrary the prohibition to be meant equally for birds when flying, the rule is practical and valuable; moreover, it is then in accordance with the principle "Cujus est solum ejus est uspue ad coelum", the generally adopted basis of the right of land-property, as we have shown in the preceding pages.

So altogether there is no reason to distinguish between birds touching or not touching the soil. But then, there neither is any reason to distinguish between birds flying high or flying less high, which would mean the introduction of a restriction that is likely greatly to hamper the effect of many provisions, a restriction, moreover, to which not the slightest allusion has been made by any law.

D. Jurisprudence.

Dicta concerning the question, whether the landowner's right extends above the soil, are as a matter of course but scarce, the airspace not having been used in such a way as yet, that a frequent collision of rights could ensue therefrom. Some cases though, on the subject exist, and the decisions given are almost without an exception favouring our view.

Acknowledgment of the landowner's right extending to the airspace, without their mentioning a possible restriction in height, is to be found in the following decisions [2]).

The Netherlands. Court of Amsterdam 27th Nov. 1883 (W. 5023).

Supreme Court. 29th Jan. 1894 (W. 6468).

Court of Heerenveen 24th Jan. 1896 (W. 6780) — indirect decision, namely in conformity with the conclusion of the public prosecutor, that upholds the opinion.

---

1) See for instance Dutch Game Law, art. 26; Loi sur la police de la chasse 3/4 m ai 1844, art. 9.
2) See for all decisions Appendix B 4.

France. Trib. corr. d'Arras 1828. Gaz. Trib. 30 oct. 1828 [1]).

    Cour de Paris 15 avr. 1864. Dalloz 1880. 3. 103.

    Trib. corr. de Corbeil. 10 déc. 1880 [2]).

    Trib. civ. de Tours. 19 janv. 1887. Dalloz 1900. 2. 361.

    Cour d'appel d'Amiens. 19 févr. 1896. Dalloz 1896. 2. 464.

    Trib. de paix de Lille 15 nov. 1899. Dalloz 1900. 3. 361.

    Cour d'appel de Lyon 9 avr. 1903. Dalloz 1906. 2. 178.

Belgium. Cassation Bruxelles 15 mai 1876. La Belg. jud. 1876. p. 602.

Switzerland. Urteilsantr. der bundesgerichtl. Commission [3]).

England and U. S. America. Lemmon v. Webb. 70 L. T. 275.

    Clifton v. Viscount of Bury. 4 T. L. R. 8.

    National Telephone Co. v. Baker. 62 L. J. Ch. 699 [4]).

    Wandsworth District Board of Works v. United Telephone Co. 13 Q. B. D. 904 (C. A.).

    Finchley Electric Light Co. v. Finchley Urban District 1902, 1 Ch. 866; 1903, 1 Ch. 437 [5]).

    Kenyon v. Hart. 34 L. J. M. C. 87 [4]).

    Murphy v. Bolger. 60 Vt. 723.

    Hoffman v. Armstrong. 48 N. Y. 201.

A curious decision concerning the connection between land and airspace has been given by in an English case. It held that a telegraph company, by establishing a telegraph line along a railway line, was liable to be rated to the poor rate in respect of the land the posts were placed in and the land covered by the wires.

    Electric Telegraph Company v. Overseers of Salford. 11 Ex. 181.

    See also Ambrose Q. C., in Lancashire Telephone Co. v. Overseers of Manchester. C. A. 14 Q. B. D. 267.

    Some judgments favour the above mentioned view that the

---

1) See Julliot. De la propriété du domaine aérien 1909, p. 10.
2) See Cirier. Du délit de chasse sur le terrain d'autrui. 1887, p. 143.
3) See Meili. Die Anwendung des Expropriationsrechtes auf die Telephonie 1888. p. 50.
4) See Engineering. June 11 1909. p. 793.

too, the condition is that the use of the airspace be essential to the use of the soil, so here again we have an affirmation of our assertion that the state rules as high as it thinks necessary.

Netherlands. Court of appeal of Amsterdam. 18 oct. 1901. W. 7682.

France. Cour de Douai 8 juin 1887. Dalloz 1896. 2. 464.

Trib. civ. de Compiègne. 19 déc. 1888. Dalloz 1900. 2. 361.

Trib. civ. de la Seine 7e Ch. 19 mai 1908 [1]).

England and U. S. America. Pickering v. Rudd. 4 Camp. 219 [2]).

Butler v. Frontier Telephone Co. 186 N. Y. 486.

Germany. Reichsgericht, Civ. Sen. 21 Sept. 1898. Entsch. des Reichsger. 42. p. 205.

Reichsger. Civ. Sen. 29 okt. 1904. Entsch. des Reichsger. Neue Folge IX, p. 116.

Austria. O. G. H. 27 Nov. 1907. Österr. Zentralbl. für die juristische Praxis, Jänner 1909. p. 33.

In opposition to this authority in our favour we found but a very modest number of decisions of a different opinion, holding that land-property only extends to what is united with the soil.

Netherlands. Supreme Court 22 Dec. 1882 (W. 4861). — Indirect decision, namely in conformity with the conclusion of the attorney general, that upholds the opinion.

Local Court of Goor 23th March 1893 (quashed Supreme Court. 29th Jan. 1894. W. 6468).

France. Cour de Douai 11 févr. 1880. Dalloz 1896. 2. 464.

Belgium. Cour d'appel de Gand. 6 déc. 1869. La Belg. jud. 1869, p. 1561.

And a close examination of these judgments shows that they are but poor arguments indeed. Two of them are Dutch and, as we have indicated, the Dutch Code was the very one whose terminology was vaguer on this point than that of the other

---

1) See Bonnefoy, l. c., p. 125.

lower judge and was quashed by the court of cassation, and the second one being an indirect decision of the court of cassation, has been followed by two judgments of that court in an opposite direction. For the same reason the Court of Douai's judgment loses much of its value, this court having seven years later, in an identical case, come round to the opinion we are defending. And as to the Belgium judgment, of the Court of Ghent, we have already seen that Belgium's highest court does not agree with the Ghent decision.

———

E. Aerial Navigation.

Last not least, aerial navigation is already beginning to be the cause of legal provisions proving our opinion to be in the right. First, on the occasion of the Tschudi balloon incident (August 1909) on the German-Russian frontier, the Russian guards were doubly blamed because of their shooting at the balloon when still soaring above German territory. And the fact of these officials shooting at aeronauts passing over the frontier (again in Aug. 1910) shows that they consider the frontier they have to guard, to extend into the air, and that it is desirable to have this point settled by the governments.

But there is more. Some years ago the council of a small town in Florida enacted a regulation [1]), saying that the boundaries of the airship limit of the town shall be held to extend upward in a vertical direction to a distance of twenty miles in the sky, and giving further regulations for the aerial traffic above the town, even adding the promise that the council shall as soon as praticable purchase an aeroplane to enable them to properly enforce the provisions of the ordinance. Likewise, the French and the German governments are preparing laws concerning national aerial intercourse, showing thereby unmistakeably that they consider themselves competent to regulate or even prohibit the use of the airspace.

How can it be denied that these projects prejudice to a high

———

1) Ordinance regulating the status and employment of airships within the town of

else can it be at present, if not a deed of sovereignty, to tell aeronauts where they may go and where not, how they are to pass each other; to prohibit, for instance, all aerial navigation above towns, except by permission of the counnil, like art. 7 of the French project?

———————

§ 4. Conclusion.

We hope this summary may be sufficient to show that jurisprudence and literature of the most important countries consider the airspace to be subject to the right of the owner of the underlying land and that on various subjects provisions have been enacted regulating interests in the air, sometimes very high in the air. Whether in private law it is preferable to speak of a right of property or of a right of use is of no consequence as we have shown. The point we wanted to prove is that sovereign states, whenever they think fit, make laws by virtue of their sovereignty, viewing many interests not connected with the soil, reaching much higher than houses and towers.

One has objected that it is unreasonable to attribute such high aspirations to those regulations, whose makers thought of no real air rules. This is by no means a strong argument; the reverse has not been meant and that is sufficient. Besides, not only the Telegraph acts and the Game acts are sure to have been made with a view to interests lying higher than houses, but especially the new codes of Germany, Switzerland and Hungary are a decisive proof against the said objection. Reckoning with aerial navigation, with the possible use of the higher regions, they have restricted the landowner's right, but they purposely leave it to the judge to decide in each concrete case, to what height the right goes. Especially the codes of Germany and of Hungary are interesting on this point, as in positive terms they start from the principle that the landowner's right extends to an unlimited height.

> B. G. B. § 905. The right of the owner of a piece of land extends to the space above the surface.
>
> Project of Code of Hungary 1st Text § 569. The right

With so many examples before us, it seems incredible that so many writers can maintain that as to the question under discussion antecedents are entirely failing. On the contrary, one cannot too strongly bear in mind that the proclamation of air-freedom would mean expulsion of the sovereign states from a domain where up till to-day they reigned as a matter of course, without any one disputing their right to do so.

Nothing, as yet, seems to intimate that the governments feel inclined in general to withdraw in behalf of aeronauts from their undisputed air-domain. Certainly one may not see a sign of an inclination in this direction in the friendly rather than hostile attitude a state takes towards aerial navigation, which attitude can only intimate the state's willingness to treat this new sort of international traffic with goodwill. Neither can we see an indication of the states being inclined to accept the principle of airfreedom in their obvious desire not to hinder wireless telegraphy more than is necessary, though Meili thinks so, confusing the two principles, concession of free international intercourse and airfreedom [1]). Meurer too seems to confuse them, though the rest of his deliberations makes it probable that with him it is but a matter of unprecise terminology, using the word airfreedom, though not meaning to refer to the fundamental principle [2]). At any rate, the term may but be used to indicate a state of freedom like that of the high seas, and not in the sense of freedom of traffic granted by the free will of the sovereign state, in which sense Meurer several times uses it. Now free passage has really been guaranteed to wireless telegraphy, but nothing more; the sovereignty question has been left untouched. As we have indicated before, this right of passage can be based on either principle; so, now that we have the conviction that states consider themselves sovereign in the air, we needs must conclude that the wireless telegraphic convention is based on the sovereign principle. The omission of any mention of the question intimates

---

1) Meili. Die Luft in ihrer Bedeutung für das modernste Verkehrs- und Transport-recht. Seuffert's Blätter für Rechtsanwendung. 1 Jan. 1909, p. 1.

should give up their air-sovereignty without a word, and by a regulation fitting either theory, being unacceptable.

We therefore conclude that state sovereignty reaches quite as high as the state's interest can reach, the possibility of which but ends at the uttermost limit of the atmosphere. Usually the space above 15000 feet is considered of too slight importance to be considered at all, because man cannot breathe there. However, as earnest technical experts even risk a prediction which to layman's ears sounds most fantastic, namely that the final success of earthly flying will be emigration from the earth, when this becomes uninhabitable [1]), it surely may not be called preposterous to suppose the possibility of oxygen apparatus enabling coming generations to navigate the higher regions. Though the chance of really frequent traffic there, seems not very great, still it is desirable to keep to the sovereignty principle also for the highest regions, as long as the possibility of any use exists.

We see, that it does not matter in the least how far artillery fire reaches, nor how far the state may be able to really control the air-domain, this being a question of practical facts. Though a state may be unable to watch over its interests high up in the air, unable to make its authority felt in every part of its air-domain, one may not conclude that sovereignty is non-existing because of that. Remote parts of the territory, too, know a like absence of control and the law of nations estimates that sovereignty is not lost on account of that [2]).

In principle the airspace belongs to the sovereign state territory, so the state has full sovereignty to an unlimited height, which sovereignty can only be abolished or restricted by treaty. If there exist such valid objections against the ground-state's sovereignty that it is desirable to take it away, or if there are perhaps some points more fit for common than for national regulation, a convention will be necessary to establish such

1) Ferber. L'Aviation, 1908, p. 161 where he names as partisans of his opinion: Wells, Esnault-Pelterie, Archdeacon, Quinton.

2) Not even as regards occupied territory. See for instance Oppenheim International Law 1905, I, p. 298; Ullmann, Völkerrecht 1908, p. 324; Hall, l. c., p. 116; Pradier-

height and, if necessary, conventions will bring such exceptions upon the right of sovereignty as the state itself allows to be made.

B. The Ground-state's Interest at Recognition of its Air-sovereignty; Objections against such Sovereignty.

Arguing that the states, when demanding recognition of their air-sovereignty have the right on their side, we looked at the subject under discussion from one side only. We examined the position of the airspace above sovereign state territory, according to existing law, and we saw that the general principles of law in this matter plead for sovereignty of the ground-state, and that the states' attitude intimates that their air-sovereignty, when needed, has never been doubted. So by now we know what is the right of the ground-state, we know that its right to reign as high above the soil as it thinks fit, can only be abolished by treaty. The other side of the question we mean to consider next is, whether it is desirable to maintain the said sovereignty. Can such sovereignty endanger other interests, interests of such supreme importance as to require the sacrifice of the ground-state's right? To answer this question we can do no better than test the desirability of air-sovereignty to the ground-state's interest in remaining sovereign and to the possible drawbacks of that sovereignty.

---

§ 1. Ground-state's Interests.

The importance the airspace has for the ground-state is on the verge of acquiring a wholly new aspect since the navigation of the air is an accomplished fact.

The chief points that seem to us especially to require the maintenance of the states' air-sovereignty are as follows:

1. General safety on the ground. First of all, the imperative interest the state has in all that is going on above its territory, since any object being there and being heavier than the air

kept up artificially at whatever altitude this may be. Meili thinks this danger of injury by means of objects dropped from above insufficient to make sovereignty necessary, though he only gives the not too convincing argument: "Indeed, one may not make aerial navigation impossible" [1].

Another nuisance for people on the ground, an impediment for the quiet enjoyment of private land-property, would be the stationing of airships in the air above such property.

2. Espionage and other hostilities. The state must be entitled to prohibit all aerial navigation in the neighbourhood of fortifications. Surely the advent of the possibility of spying from the skies will bring about a radical change in the technics of fortifications. But let it be ever so little, there will probably be something to spy for a long time yet to come.

3. Smuggling. If the state can find a way to enforce its customs also towards airships flying over the earthly frontiers, it must without doubt have the right to do so.

4. Infection. Again, if a state is able to enforce quarantine measures in the air above its territorial frontiers, or above its territory, it must have the authority to make and enforce such measures, for the presence of infected aircraft above a country is no doubt a menacing danger. And the state of the future will certainly have to watch against infection in the air as well as on the land.

5. Police. The advent of aerial navigation suggests a new means to burglars and the like, of coming unnoticed and of disappearing without leaving a trace behind them. Therefore a well organised air police will be an imperative necessity for the state of the future.

6. Science. Airships may be a great nuisance to astronomers. For the sake of science the state must be entitled to prohibit temporarily or locally all aerial navigation, or the stationing of airships, as the case may be.

7. Light and warmth. It is often said that the ground-state

---

1) Meili. Das Luftschiff im internen Recht und Völkerrecht, 1908, p. 28.

must needs have sovereignty over the airspace since the air is the medium through which light and warmth reach the earth. We fail to see the value of this argument. Light and warmth are indispensable to the state, to be sure; but seriously, who expects such a crowd of airships and flying machines that the sun will be darkened by them? The argument can only be of some value for countries having those installations that catch the heat of the sun in order to make this natural force useful; for instance, by concentrating the sun's rays by means of a hollow glass on a hot-air motor. The working of such installations which do exist in very dry and hot parts in the West of the United States of America, would indeed be greatly hampered if airships were allowed to be stationed between the glass and the sun. However, the climate of most countries especially of Europe, being absolutely unfit for installations of the kind, this special interest cannot be called a universal one. Perhaps coming generations will discover a means to accumulate the heat of the sun and to keep this force in store till they want it. Then, of course, the case becomes quite different; then for all countries the protection of these installations against possible hindrance from airships will be of eminent interest. So the possibility of utilising the force of the sun's rays in this way can count as a conditional interest.

8. Trade. Trade in the future will be partly carried on in the air, which involves that the safety of the airway must be guaranteed. If the airspace of a country is known to be unsafe, air-trade companies are sure to avoid connections with such a country. So for trade's sake again, the state wants authority over the airspace.

To defend all these numerous special interests nothing short of full sovereignty will suffice. Reason enough indeed to establish this right if it were not existing. How much more so then to maintain it where it does exist! The state's existence, its prosperity, its development, all are narrowly connected with

own eyes, according to its own views of right and safety. If
not, the safety and the welfare of the territory itself will be
most precarious.

---

§ 2. Objections.

Enumerating the objections against the ground-state's sovereignty over the airspace is soon done, since the only interest
that is said to be endangered by our theory is international
airtraffic. Being sovereign, the state can make laws and rules
impeding or even forbidding aerial navigation. Fearing such
rules and hoping to escape them, quite a number of authors
conclude that air-sovereignty has not to be recognised at all, or
but in a limited way. We are of opinion that most people are inclined to take the part of the aeronauts rather too much. For why
indeed are we to favour air-travellers so much above land-travellers?
Why are we to guarantee them that, till the end of the world,
they will be free to draw in the air as many circles and other
figures as they like? The more the airway is used, the more
hindrances for aeronauts will ensue; this is inevitable. The
denser the population, the busier the traffic, the more rules
are needed to secure order and safety; but there is no reason
whatever to call such necessary rules a wilful impediment of
international intercourse. This is true for traffic in general, so
also for the particular new kind through the air. If a state
makes provisions to protect people and territory against injuries
by means of airships and flying machines, if it wants to reserve
part of its airspace for special exercises or observations, if it
thinks necessary to prohibit all aerial navigation above fortifications and if therefore it tells aeronauts to fly a short way
about, there is not the slightest reason for complaints. Some
restricting provisions are sure to be made not only under the
sovereignty theory, but they will be quite as well necessary
under the freedom theory. It would be unreasonable indeed to
insist on the ground-state's rights and interests being sacrified
to the leisure of aeronauts, the more so since nothing intimates
that their moral standard will be as high above that of land

reasonable claim: airtraffic must not stand behind landtraffic. Now there is reason enough to believe that modern states are not inclined to be against progress. But to promote the development of international airtraffic we need neither the sacrifice of the ground-state's sovereignty, nor a restriction of its sovereignty by means of a servitude of free passage, as international traffic on land clearly shows us. The same principle of equality concerning foreigners or inhabitants that is generally adopted on the land, is sure to be extended to the air-domain. So in this respect aerial intercourse no doubt will have as good a chance to reach a high degree of international development as the intercourse on land.

The result of our considerations is that the ground-state's right and interest both plead for full sovereignty and that but little, very little indeed can be said against our solution. Considering the diversity of solutions proposed, and the great importance of the matter, we think it desirable that a clear statement on this point should be made. Among the numerous advantages the system offers, we name:

1. Airtraffic will be sufficiently free.

2. It avoids the difficulty of deciding the altitude of a horizontal frontier.

3. States are maintained in their present juridical position in respect of the airspace.

4. They can watch over the welfare of their subjects and of their territory according to their own opinion.

5. They are, as a matter of course, competent to regulate eventual new interests.

6. They grant international airtraffic concessions if they think necessary, which implies a far worthier attitude than other solutions bring to the state, granting it only some conventional rights.

CHAPTER II.

CONSEQUENCES OF THE SOVEREINGTY THEORY.

SECTION I. LIMITED SOVEREIGNTY.

The theory extending the authority of the sovereign state to the airspace above the territory, involves as a first consequence that, where the surface of the globe is without a sovereign master, the airspace overhead has no sovereign either. Thus, above the open sea and above land as yet unoccupied the space is free. Thus far there is no difficulty in applying the principle that the airspace belongs to the land beneath it. But there are many other cases where the application may be less simple, we mean those cases where the sovereignty of the groundstate is more or less limited. There the question may arise as to whether such limitations include the air-domain or not. We should say that as a rule it all depends on the meaning of the stipulations, though some general indications may be given on the matter.

---

§ 1. States Partly Dependent on Other States.

Among the states with limited sovereignty are, first of all, to be classed the partly dependent states, that are conventionally obliged to suffer foreign interference in their affairs on some points. Generally such restrictions of sovereignty will concern the airspace as well as the land, as far as they can have a practical effect in the air. For as the air-domain forms a part of the state, it shares as a matter of course all restrictions

and so on [1]).

There is no difficulty until we get to restrictions viewing special parts or points of the land, or special situations. In such cases it may be difficult to know whether the meaning of the restriction makes it desirable to include the air-domain. At any rate one must be very careful not to conclude hastily to a large interpretation, not to extend to the air restrictions which have been obviously meant for situations on the ground, and the more so because the limitations are concessions of the dependent state under reservation of all its other rights.

Thus the right of military occupation can, for instance, in some cases give rise to difficulties of interpretation. If the right is given in very general terms, so as to regard the whole state domain, it includes the air-domain as part of the state. If, on the contrary, the stipulation is not general, we must distinguish between the different cases. In case the right has been given in respect of a special region, a province, the airspace above will as a rule have to share the restriction, being an appurtenance of that part of the territory. But if the right concerns the occupation of a certain point having a special strategic value, such as a mountain-pass, or a bridge, or a fortification, the treaty does not mean to allow the occupation of a part of the state, but it only gives a right for a very special purpose. This purpose being in most cases connected with acts on the ground excludes extension into the air. We say in most cases, for the contrary, too, is possible. For instance, the right of occupying some fortifications along a part of the frontier is obviously given to guard the state there against foreign invasion and this certainly cannot be effective unless it implies the right of control in the air as well.

A restriction one can call in a sense the reverse of the right of occupation is the interdiction of maintaining military forces. Of this we find a striking example in the case of Montenegro. Art. 29 of the Berlin Treaty of July 13th 1878 says that Montenegro must abstain from the possession of a naval force

---

1) See for instance the treaties between France and Annam (6th June 1884) and

Will military airships, hovering over the sea, where vessels of war may not come, be tolerated? The great difficulty of finding a satisfactory solution lies in the fact that, airships being able to manœuvre as well above the land as above the sea, it will be impossible to draw a line between air forces above land or above sea. The treaty evidently wants to forbid the participation in a maritime war, the guarding of the sea frontier, in short any display of power on the sea. Until to-day this could be guaranteed by the existing prohibition. But no sooner will aerial navigation find its application to warfare, than this interdiction will be insufficient. Even if one takes the meaning of the restriction, which wants to prevent any display of power in the sea-regions, there cannot be the same certainty as to the interdiction being efficacious in future. For to have that certainty, one must prohibit not only the possession of an aerial naval force, but that of any air-machine, the difference between air force above land and above sea on one hand, and between military air-machines and others on the other hand, not being so great as to prevent a very easy transformation. To prohibit all aerial navigation is, of course, beyond the meaning of the treaty, and so is certainly the interdiction to have military airships, for this would imply a new restriction, as it would deprive the land forces of the chance of being assisted by airships.

The interdiction of having a naval airflag will be impracticable in the not improbable case that airflag above land and airflag above sea are proclaimed to be one and the same. For in that case, to have an airflag above land will imply the possession of the airflag above sea. Then the only alternative to be adopted will be the prohibition of displaying aerial power and airflag above the sea. But this is a far less efficacious restriction than the present one.

Quite another class of examples of restrictions, which are apt to give rise to difficulties, is to be found in treaties guaranteeing the freedom of commercial intercourse with a country or with some ports. For instance, the protectorate treaty between France and Annam [1]), allows trade with but a few ports of the

terms; obviously it is meant for foreign trade in its largest sense. Not only the port as a waterway, but all the town is open to that trade and to the establishments it involves. Trade by air must, therefore, be considered to be free as well as trade by sea, though one must bear in mind this is not that the concession concerning a river or a port must include the space above it, but because air-trade is a special means of trade in general.

A similar example is to be found in the Congo Convention. This Convention declares, as largely as possible, the trade of all nations to be free in the basin of the Congo and its surroundings [1]). Although the articles that elaborate the principle do not, of course, mention air-trade, the general articles which give the principle leave no room for the slightest doubt that all sorts of trade are meant, no matter by what means. One cannot, therefore, exclude the trade by air. More restricted are the articles that establish the faculties of the Congo Commission. They show too clearly that the makers were thinking only of the existing ways of trading for them to be applicable to air-trade [2]). So here a little addition seems desirable, as the spirit of the Convention must certainly lead to the subjection of airtrade to the control of the Congo Commission.

----

§ 2. Real Union and Federal State.

A second category of states lacking part of their sovereignty are the states forming a real union or a federal state. Both cases show us a territory where two sorts of authority are exercised, sometimes that of the state as a unity, sometimes that of the composing parts separately. To mark the line between these two sorts of authority is the task of the constitution and suppletory conventions, and likewise these documents will have to be consulted concerning the division of authority in respect of the air-domain of such states. No

----
1) Gen. Act of the Berlin Conf. 26th Febr. 1885, Art. 1—5.

Again, the general rules will be applied without difficulty to the air-domain. For instance, the defence is, generally speaking, a matter of the competence of the central government; the air-defence will be so too, without contest. Another example: the constitution of Switzerland (art. 8) confers on the federal government the almost exclusive faculty of contracting treaties. So treaties concerning the airspace, though surely the possibility of their existence has not been in the minds of the makers of the constitution, are as a matter of course included in the faculty.

Again, it is the more special rules that may prove to be a source of difficulties. Several of them will need reviewing as a simple example may show. The Swiss Constitution says in art. 13 that if a canton wants to maintain more than 300 soldiers, it needs the permission of the federal government. Will this article be of any influence if a canton decides to maintain a military airship, manned by part of the 300 soldiers? Or can it act without asking leave? The article's redaction is clear and literally no objection, and the constitution, moreover, reserves (art. 3) to the cantons any right it does not give explicitly to the federal government. But the spirit of the article is clearly to assure the control of the central government over the extension of the means of defence.

A provision of a like nature is to be found in the Constitution of the United States of America. No state, it says [1]), may maintain in time of peace military forces or men-of-war. Here the interdiction is put sharper, leaving no doubt as to its intention being to interdict the possession of any means of defence.

In both cases the meaning seems to be broader than the redaction and will probably make provision necessary.

———

All these examples may have shown that the effect of many

---

[1]) Const. U. S. A. Art. I, Sec. 10, par. 3.

there are numbers of treaties which, though considered not to impair sovereignty in the least, do involve in reality a slight diminution of the liberty of action of the states concerned, inasmuch as these have bound themselves by the treaties. These, too, may be dubious as to their extent.

Wherever there is doubt one will have to examine the meaning of the treaty to make out whether alteration or completion is necessary or desirable.

---

§ 3. Maritime Belt.

Concerning the airspace above the maritime belt our theory is not likely to give any difficulty. Though the nature of the state's authority in respect of the maritime belt is a moot point [1]), the amount of that authority is a pretty well settled matter. The position of the airspace above the maritime belt makes it desirable to consider that space to be subject to a like amount of authority, and we should say there is no obvious objection against this solution. The right of innocent passage, regarding only navigation, does not include the passage by air, but as a like right can be as useful to aerial navigation as it is to navigation, it seems but rational that the states will tolerate such passage through this aerial belt as well.

---

§ 4. International Rivers and Canals.

The condition of the international rivers and canals is peculiar enough to require some special consideration. In the general opinion these rivers and canals remain under the sovereignty of the riparian state except the concessions made to international navigation. Can these concessions affect the sovereignty concerning the airspace above the rivers and canals? It is obvious that they only regard navigation and may not be

---

1) De Lapradelle, Le droit de l'état sur la mer territoriale R. D. I. P. 1898, p. 264
Sohücking, Das Küstenmeer, 1897.
Visser, De territoriale zee, Utrecht 1894.

aerial navigation can but occasionally have to do with such rules. To give an example: the convention of navigation of the Rhine [1] establishes a special jurisdiction for damage done by vessels navigating the Rhine. An airship can, of course, be the damaged object and if that is so, the case is of the competence of the special judge of the Rhine. However, this is clearly but a quite occasional necessity, by no means placing the whole airspace above the river under his jurisdiction. The concession has been given for the navigation of the waterway and nothing beyond that. Another example we find in a stipulation concerning the Danube. This, too, is sure to affect aerial navigation but the case is somewhat different. In the Berlin Treaty of 1878 [2] we find an interdiction to maintain men-of-war on that river. Here surely, some extension into the air will be necessary, for the meaning of the interdiction seems not to agree with military airships hovering just above the Danube. But again this is an example of a single provision needing extension into the air, all the regulations taken as a whole concern the navigation of the river and have nothing to do with the airspace.

The Suez Canal Convention [3] again concerns only the navigation of the canal, though again some acts in the air will be affected by it. The first article of the Convention lays down in general terms the obligation not to interfere with the free use of the canal, and this surely can regard acts in the air. For instance, acts of hostility above the canal can be as great a hindrance to the free use of the canal as the acts of hostility art. IV prohibits to take place on the canal; so they are in flat defiance of art. I; art. IV referring to vessels only is no objection, as art. I gives the principle. But again, it must be remembered that this influence is but occasional, there can be no question of considering the airspace to be a part of the canal, as the object of the treaty. The purpose of the concession is to establish

---

1) Convention révisée pour la navigation du Rhin, 17 Oct. 1868, art. 34.
2) Treaty of Berlin. July 13th 1878, art. 52.
3) International Convention for securing the free navigation of the Suez Canal

A question connected with this convention would be: is it desirable to establish a like concession for aerial navigation? Commercial aircraft will hardly care for the right of passage above the canal, as aerial intercourse very likely will be granted over all countries, and a special way of passage will be wholly unnecessary in consequence. But military airships may be pretty well sure to be in need of such a passage. Even in time of peace their freedom of traverse will not be so great as that of commercial airships, and in time of war the air-domain of neutral states will be neutral domain, that is closed to the belligerents. The powers that were very anxious to get the Suez Canal because of their interests in the far East, will not be able to do in the long run without a similar communication for their airforces. Now airships need no special way to be made for them, they only want a concession of passage. Having no such concession they may perhaps feel tempted to violate the rights of Egypt. To prevent such violation of the sovereignty of Egypt and in time of war more especially of its neutrality, it seems advisable to establish a similar concession of passage in respect of aerial navigation. Of course, there is no necessity to take the very space above the Suez Canal for this concession, but the spot seems extremely fit for it, and, moreover, it seems to be the simplest way, to establish the right by a slight alteration of the existing convention.

SECTION II. EXTENSION OF SOVEREIGNTY OUTSIDE THE STATE DOMAIN.

§ 1. Aircraft Outside the State Domain.

All ships on the seas, beyond the territorial limits of any state, are considered to be subject to the sovereignty of the state to which they belong. Air-machines being in similar conditions are sure to be treated in the same way. But when coming into the domain of a foreign state, the vessel of war's position is different from that of the merchant vessel. As to

great difference between navigation and aerial navigation will perhaps lead to different consequences.

A. Military Aircraft.

Especially the position of aerial military forces will be difficult to define. Air forces being able to hover above every part of the territory and to approach the foreign state from every side, on the land frontier as well as on the sea frontier, are in a position widely differing from that of the naval forces, and cannot therefore claim the same treatment. The sharp division in aerial force above land and aerial force above sea is impracticable. The conditions above land are often the same as above the sea, at other times they are different again in both cases. Consequently, one is obliged to examine the different eventualities and decide accordingly.

Men-of-war are as a rule admitted into foreign ports in time of peace, though they are subject to any conditions the state thinks fit to annex to the admission. This hospitality is chiefly founded on the wants of navigation, it is a service states render each other, but which they are fully entitled to refuse. Aerial navigation can no better do without landing from time to time than navigation can. Consequently, if an airship is coming from the side of the sea, it is in a like position as a vessel of war, both coming from the free international maritime highway, both needing a landing place, and both lacking the occasion to land on national territory. So there seems to be good reasons to claim a like hospitality for air forces as that which the naval forces enjoy.

Wholly different, however, is the case when we think of a military airship asking hospitality on the land frontier. Since states will probably not be very keen on having foreign airships manœuvring above their territory, the air-domain is likely to be closed to foreign air forces. But then the desire to land on foreign territory can only exist in these two cases: either one is quite near the frontier but still on the national side of

must be to steer to the national territory. There is no reason for any exceptional hospitality here. We say: unless in case of distress, because this is the one case in which asylum is considered by international usage a right that may not be refused.

In respect of the air forces the appreciation of distress will again be different according to the case presenting itself either on the sea frontier or on the land frontier. For on the sea frontier there is distress as soon as there is necessity of going down, since one has no choice of landing anywhere but on that one country which is at hand. On the land frontier, however, the necessity of going down does not imply the necessity of landing on the foreign side of the frontier. Not until this necessity exists too, can the case be considered to be distress, so as to make hospitality a duty.

Besides these cases states are not likely to object to occasional special permission of access into the air-domain; for instance, for the purpose of simple passage, or of an official visit to the country.

In all these cases foreign air forces will be in about the same position as men-of-war in a foreign port. They likewise represent the sovereign authority of the state and, as such, they are entitled to similar privileges as those conceded to vessels of war; but on the other hand, they have also a rather menacing character and, as such, they will surely be subject to rather severe conditions.

B. Merchant Aircraft.

To merchant air-machines access into the foreign air-domain will certainly be granted in normal circumstances. Can it be called necessary to let these visitors remain under the penal competence of the state under whose flag they are flying, which has been proposed by Meurer? [1]) We think not. Rightly Collard [2]) has objected to this theory that it does not fit into Meurer's system of sovereignty to an unlimited height, and that,

1) Meurer l. c. p. 33.

can come to a very satisfactory solution though starting from the territorial principle.

Adhering to the principle of the ground-state's sovereignty, we think it preferable by far to declare the jurisdiction of the ground-state to be the prevailing one in the air, though with some rational exceptions.

In imitation of the French doctrine most states are ready nowadays [1]) to consider foreign merchant vessels when staying in their ports, to be exempt from their jurisdiction in respect of acts of interior discipline, and of crimes committed by the officers and the crew between themselves, as long as the peace of the port is not disturbed. It seems rational and simple to apply this system to air-machines in foreign air-domain. The aforesaid acts, when committed on board an airship, cannot greatly matter to the ground-state as long as the peace, the order, the safety of the state, do not suffer by it. Moreover, the concession will be a lighter one where airships are concerned than in respect of vessels. First, airships, and the like, can take but a few persons and secondly, they are not dwellings like ships, so a situation similar to the lying at anchor in a port is not very likely to be realisable in the near future in the air. The extension of the privilege to the crew, when landing for purposes connected with the service, cannot, therefore, be of any value either, since the tie between the crew and the balloon or flying machine is broken and the principle, not being a personal one, stops being of value, as soon as they are put aside in the shed.

There is another reason why it is desirable to accept some exceptions on the competence of the ground-state. We must first of all try to get as much guarantee as possible that for every wrong there can be had redress. If possible, there may not be cases, where the competent judge cannot be indicated. Now in the air we can have the very special case that even

---

1) Bonfils. Manuel de droit intern. publ. 1908, p. 381.
Perels. Das intern. öffentl. Seerecht der Gegenwart 1903, p. 61.
Wheaton. Elements of International Law, (Atlay) 1904 p. 166.

the state in whose domain a crime has been committed, cannot be identified. Aeronauts flying at full speed in lonely high regions may safely be supposed to know moments in which the identity of the underlying land is uncertain to them. The territorial competence being in such cases insufficient, that of the home state imposes itself as a satisfactory completion.

A similar uncertainty may be imagined likewise in respect of acts concerning several air-machines. Say, a collision takes place high up in the air, whilst underlying clouds or mist take away the opportunity of distinguishing the land below and no other airships are in sight; a collision which is the fault of an aeronaut who does not show any flag or number. In the territorial system it would be often impossible to come in such a case to a satisfactory solution. For the damaged aeronaut would have to chose between these two: either go down, thereby finding out the identity of the state, but letting the culprit escape; or follow the latter and thereby never knowing the name of the state, unless he be able to define with instruments the exact spot where the deed was committed. Airships can carry with them such instruments as are wanted for this, but even then there can be uncertainty, namely, if one has not used them immediately, and especially if the spot was near a frontier. On board flying machines, however, it is according to technical experts impossible to take, and anyhow to use, these instruments.

Exclusive competence of the ground-state, we conclude, would lead in many cases to impossibility of getting redress. Therefore, in all such cases where the identity of the ground-state is uncertain, there needs must be a substitute competence, for instance, that of the state of the damaged airship.

———

C. Airspace Above Vessels.

In consequence of the theory that vessels on the high seas and men-of-war in foreign ports are regarded as floating parts of their home state [1]) one has suggested that this could affect

———
1) Calvo. Le droit intern. théorique et pratique I, p. 552; III, p. 337.

is territory, the space above it is above state territory, consequently subject to that state's sovereignty. However, there is no reason to accept this. The so-called exterritoriality of the ship is only a fiction, by means of which one wants to say that in certain respects ships will be treated as if they were floating parts of the territory, but this does not make them so in reality. The fiction wants to say that the ship will be treated as if she were at home. At home ships are not territory, so in another part of the world the mere fact that they are considered to be at home, cannot make them territory either. The exterritoriality is nothing more than a name, trying to picture the position of the ship in two words; it is not the juridical basis of that position and cannot, therefore, be the source of other rights.

Besides, there is a practical objection against letting the privilege concern the whole airspace above the ship. Evidently, it would be rational to decide in a like manner where airships and the airspace above them are concerned. But then, it will often occur that airships are floating above vessels of another nationality, which means that part of the airspace above the vessel will be the same as the space above the airship, which means again that there would be two claims of sovereignty in respect of that part of the airspace. Then, which sovereignty is to be regarded prevalent?

---

§ 2. Ambassador's Residence.

A similar suggestion to the aforesaid will perhaps be made concerning the other case of so-called exterritoriality, the ambassador's residence. The inviolability of his house is among the most important privileges of the ambassador's. The old theory, calling the house exterritorial, regarding it as being really part of the home state's territory, could involve this consequence, that the space above must be part of the home state,

to its being short and expressive. Here, again, it is no more than a short name for some existing privileges, not their juridical basis. So, again, this name cannot be the source of new rights.

Neither is there any necessity to extend the privilege to the airspace. The reason of the right is, that one wants to guarantee the ambassador a place where, with his family, his suite and his papers, he is free from the local authority. This is considered a necessary consequence of the inviolability of his person, which again is essential to him, in order to fulfil the duties of his mission. Now all this seems to be quite sufficiently served by the existing privilege. The only extension aerial navigation can lead to is that perhaps eventual air equipages will be inserted in the privilege, just as land equipages share it.

SECTION III. CONSEQUENCES AS TO THE LAWS OF WAR.

§ 1. The Theatre of War.

Modern law of nations allows acts of war to take place only within the territory of the belligerents or on the high seas. If air forces are allowed to engage in future wars, they too will have to observe this principle, they will be limited to the air-domain of the belligerents and to the free parts of the airspace.

---

§ 2. Air-domain of Neutral States.

The great importance of the aforesaid rule lies in its complement, which forbids acts of hostility within neutral territory. Hence the airspace of neutral states will be closed to hostilities. In our theory this is but logical. But, moreover, the necessity of excluding the whole airspace above neutral territory from

---

1) Institut de droit intern. Annuaire XI, p. 402, XII, p. 262 XIV, p. 241.
Pradier-Fodéré, Cours de droit diplomatique, 1881, II, p. 72.
François Pietri, Etude critique sur la fiction d'exterritorialité, 1895.
César Droin, L'exterritorialité des agents diplomatiques, 1895.
Bonfils. l. c.. p. 417.

partisans of the principle of airfreedom abandon their theory at this special point [1]). For in their system the free airspace above neutral territory ought to be part of the theatre of war, but the certainty of damage to the underlying land that would ensue from their theory, makes them acknowledge the state's neutrality to an indefinite height. Thereby they recognise one of the strongest arguments against the freedom principle. The state's evident interest as to all that is going on in the space above its territory is the very reason why that special part of the airspace can never be common property, though this interest may be more obvious in time of war than in time of peace.

And the principle is abandoned quite easily too. Meili, for instance, gives only this argument for the solution which, being in his system evidently inconsequent, demands sound motives: "Of this there can be no doubt". —

The general principle is, as we said, that the neutrality of the space above neutral territory must be respected as strictly as that of the territory. The question is, can we use for this purpose the existing rules of neutrality? The great difficulty lies in the fact that the principles of neutrality distinguish between land warfare and maritime warfare. Must we choose and apply either the land laws or the maritime laws to the air-domain? Must the state of the air-domain be a state of the strictest neutrality like that of neutral land, or must the indulgence the law of nations shows towards belligerent naval forces be extended to air forces? To answer this question we must examine the motives of this indulgence and see whether they apply to the air forces.

The important exceptions consist in this that for belligerent vessels of war it is not considered a violation of neutrality to pass through neutral maritime territory, nor to enter neutral ports and get provisioned and to a certain extent repaired there, if the neutral states allow them to.

---

1) Fauchille, l. c., p. 25.
Meili, Das Luftschiff im internen Recht und Völkerrecht 1908, p. 52.

territorial waters is chiefly founded on the fact that the maritime belt constitutes a part of the sea as international highway. Now the space above the maritime belt constitutes a transition from the free part of the airspace to the part which is not free, hence the neutral state will perhaps be less inclined to grant the passage to air forces because of their great ability to pass from above the maritime belt to the space above the land. However, this is a consideration concerning the individual neutral state. The right to allow the passage must be the same, we should say, as to the maritime belt and as to the space above it, the juridical position of both being the same, and both being one with the free transmarine international highway.

Of extending the right to the whole air-domain of neutral states, there can be no question. Maintenance of strict neutrality on the soil is so narrowly connected with maintenance of the aerial neutrality above the soil, that in both cases we must conclude to an equally strict observance. So passage above the neutral land cannot be allowed any more than it is permitted on the soil. One has objected that the right of passage above neutral land is of an imperative necessity [1]). Without this right, one says, belligerents would not be able to reach each other's air-domain, air forces would be useless as a means of war. We fail to see that this is an argument in the modern law of neutrality. Exactly the same could be said to prove that the land forces need the right of passage through neutral territory. If two lands — not neighbors — cannot reach each other by sea, there can be no war between them. Such is the inevitable consequence of the existing law of neutrality. Why should this consequence be unacceptable when applied to the air forces? If it is deemed impossible in the air, one will be obliged to alter the land rules on this point — and one will have attacked one of the leading principles of the law of neutrality.

---

1) Fauchille, l. c., p. 25.

their ports for a fixed short time, and to execute slight reparations and take in provisions. This exception to the severe principle is again based on the necessities of navigation and on the free and international character of the sea as highway. On the sea frontier similar deliberations may be held in favour of the air forces. They, too, will strongly feel the necessity of such a privilege. When coming from the free airspace above the sea, that is from regions where they have free access and where they have beneath them the same capricious sea that bears the vessels of war, there is certainly good reason to show them some indulgence.

The great difference between ships and aircraft will demand regulations which are different from those concerning maritime warfare, arrested by the second Peace Conference [1]), but the principles must be the same. So the neutral state will be free to open its coast or part of it to the belligerents, or to forbid all access — except in the case of real distress. It will be free to allow aeronauts to have small reparations carried out, and to take in provisions to a certain extent. The distinction to be made between reparations allowed and not allowed will, probably, give rise to practical difficulties. As to ships, reparation of a wholly unseaworthy ship is considered to be not allowed; but were air-machines are concerned damage is much sooner sufficient to bring about such a desolate state. The question of the provisions is likely to be a controversy too; in maritime law it has been so for a long time and even the second Hague Conference has not yet brought the question to an end, satisfactory to all nations. Rules — different again in their details from the maritime rules — will be necessary in order to fix the conditions on which the entrance, the sojourn, etc. are dependent.

All these regulations must observe the general principle that the neutral state may on no account assist the belligerents. Both belligerent parties are to be treated equally, and one

---

1) Convention respecting the rights and duties of neutral powers in naval war.

must try to arrange things in a way that leaves the opportunity to abuse the exceptional privilege as little as possible.

On the land frontiers the neutral state must again be severe. For there the air forces of the belligerents do not come from regions where landing was impossible but simply not desirable. There, landing on neutral territory will mean evasion from the enemy, either out of the enemy's air-domain, or out of one's own air-domain pursued or menaced by the enemy. At any rate, the case will bear very great similarity with that of troops crossing the neutral frontier. Now troops are as a rule not turned out in such a case, but they are interned, disarmed, not allowed to take part in the war any more. A like treatment imposes itself to be applied to the air forces asking hospitality on the land frontier. Only in case of real distress [1]) one can again make an exception, as the very special capricious nature of the air element shows itself above the land quite as well as above the sea, and constitutes a circumstance, which really pleads for an exception to the severe principle.

———

C. Permanent Neutrality.

The airspace being part of the state domain neutralisation of a territory comprises, generally speaking, the air-domain. If the neutralisation means to place a barrier between some states in order to prevent conflicts, such as is the case, for instance, with the zone on the frontier between Sweden and Norway [2]) and partly also with Belgium and Switzerland, it is obvious that this idea cannot be realised unless the neutrality extends to an unlimited height. However, there may be other cases where the necessity of complete neutrality of the air-domain seems doubtful. Neutralisation of a special point may be deemed desirable for strategic reasons which do not apply to the airspace, but view situations and acts on the soil. Again, all depends on the intention of the stipulations. To give a single example we refer to the neutralisation of the isles of Corfu and the situation of the isles opposite the Adriatic Sea. It wants to prevent the isles being fortified and their being used as a basis for acts of hostility. Can it be called necessary for the working of this neutralisation to observe the strictest neutrality as to the airspace above the isles? If Greece is at war, the Greek air-domain part of the theatre of war, there seems to be no obvious reason to call the mere passage above the isles a violation of neutrality.

———————

Literature References belonging to Chapter I Sec. I § 1.
(See p. 11—14).

Graf ZEPPELIN. Die Eroberung der Luft. 1908, pag. 28.

HENRY WHEATON. Elements of International Law. Edition Beresford Atlay 1904, pag. 292.

Dr. J. C. BLUNTSCHLI. Das moderne Völkerrecht der civilisirten Staten. 1868. Eintleitung, pag. 25.

P. PRADIER—FODÉRÉ. Traité d edroit international public. 1885. II, pag. 431.

Dr. STEPHAN. Weltpost und Luftschiffahrt. 1874, pag. 73.

ERNEST NYS. Annuaire de l'Institut de droit international. XIX, pag. 108.

OPINION OF THE INSTITUTE. Ann. de l'Inst. de dr. intr. XXI, pag 305.

Dr. J. STRANZ. Deutsche Juristenzeitung 1908, pag. 952.

Dr. F. MEILI. Das Luftschiff im internen Recht und Völkerrecht. 1908.

    Die Luft in ihrer Bedeutung für das modernste Verkehrs- und Transportrecht SEUFFERT's Blätter für Rechtsanwendung 1 Jan. 1909, pag. 1.

    Das Luftschiff und die Rechtswissenschaft. Blätter für vergleichende Rechtswissenschaft und Volkswirtschaftslehre. Febr. 1909, pag. 238.

    Die Luftschiffahrt und das Recht. Die Zukunft 24 Apr. 1909, pag 121.

FRANTZ DESPAGNET. Cours de droit international public. 1905, pag. 437.

PAUL FAUCHILLE. Le domaine aérien et le régime juridique des aérostats. 1901.

    Annuaire de l'Inst. de dr. int. XIX, pag. 19.

    Interview in „Les Sports" 3 janv. 1908. (See Bonnefoy, Le Code de l'Air. 1909, pag. 207).

L. ROLLAND. La télégraphie sans fil et le droit des gens. R. D. I. P. 1906, pag 58.

GASTON BONNEFOY. Le Code de l'Air. 1909.

A. MÉRIGNHAC. Les lois et coutumes de la guerre sur terre. 1903, pag. 196.

    Traité de droit public international II, pag. 398.

L. OPPENHEIM. International Law. 1905 I, pag. 223.

F. FERBER. L'Aviation. 1908, pag. 153.

T. MEYER. Enkele beschouwingen over luchtscheepvaart, oorlog en neutraliteit. Militairrechtelijk Tijdschrift. Maart 1909, pag. 453.

G. VAN TETS. Eenige opmerkingen naar aanleiding van de Nederlandsche Neutraliteitsproclamaties uit den laatsten tijd. Leiden 1909, pag. 195.

Prof. Dr. FRANTZ VON HOLTZENDORFF. Handbuch des Völkerrechts. 1887. II, pag. 230.

Dr. A. RIVIER. Principes du droit des gens 1896. I, pag. 140.

A. CHRÉTIEN. Principes de droit international publ. 1893, pag. 118.

FRANÇOIS PIETRI. Etude critique sur la fiction d'exterritorialité. 1895. Avant-propos, pag. 14.

Dr. HILTY. Die völkerrechtlichen Gebräuche in der atmosphärischen Zone. Archiv für öffentliches Recht 1905, pag. 87.

VON BAR. Annuaire de l'Inst. de dr. intern. XXI, pag. 304.

VON LISZT. Das Völkerrecht 1902, pag. 72.

    Das Völkerrecht 1906, pag. 80.

Dr. GRUNWALD. Luftschiffahrt und geltendes Recht. Das Recht 10 Dez. 1907, pag. 1459.

    Das Luftschiff in völkerrechtlicher und strafrechtlicher Beziehung. 1908.

    Der Luftraum in rechtlicher Beziehung zu den Teilen der Erde, über denen er sich
        befindet. Archiv für öffentliches Recht. XXIV, pag. 190.

CHRISTIAN MEURER. Luftschiffahrtsrecht. 1909.

A. MEYER. Die Erschliessung des Luftraumes in ihren rechtlichen Folgen. 1909.

    Quelques points du droit aérien. Revue juridique internationale de la locomotion
        aérienne. févr. 1910. p. 37.

Dr. E. VON ULLMANN. Völkerrecht. 1908, pag. 289.

Mr. W. L. A. COLLARD. Beschouwingen over de rechtsverhouding van de luchtruimte
        tot den staat, boven welks grondgebied zij zich verheft. Themis 1908, pag. 393.

    Weekblad van het Recht 8840.

Prof. S. GEMMA. Nuovi appunti e discussioni di diritto bellico. Rivista di diretto inter-
        nazionale 1907. Gennaio-Aprile, pag. 80.

The Solicitors' Journal and Weekly Reporter 53, pag. 209.

SIMEON E. BALDWIN. The Law of the Air-ship. The American Journal of international
        law. Jan. 1910, p. 95.

Literature, Law and Jurisprudence References belonging to Chapter I Sec. III § 3.

---

1. Provisions of Private Law concerning the Extent of Land-property (See p. 34, 35).

CODE CIVIL, art. 552.

> La propriété du sol emporte la propriété du dessus et du dessous.

DUTCH CIVIL CODE, art. 626.

> The property of the soil includes the property of what is on and in the soil.

BÜRGERL. GESETZBUCH FÜR DAS DEUTSCHE REICH, § 905.

> Das Recht des Eigenthümers eines Grundstücks erstreckt sich auf den Raum über der Oberfläche und auf den Erdkörper unter der Oberfläche.
>
> Der Eigenthümer kann jedoch Einwirkungen nicht verbieten, die in solcher Höhe oder Tiefe vorgenommen werden, dass er an der Ausschliessung kein Interesse hat

ALLGEMEIN BÜRGERL. GESETZBUCH FÜR DAS KAISERTHUM ÖSTERREICH, § 297.

> Ebenso gehören zu den unbeweglichen Sachen diejenigen, welche auf Grund und Boden in der Absicht aufgeführt werden, dass sie stets darauf bleiben sollen, als: Häuser und andere Gebäude mit dem in senkrechter Linie darüber befindlichen Luftraume.

ENTWURF DES UNGARISCHEN ALLG. BÜRG. GESETZB. Erster Text 1900, § 569.

> Das Recht des Grundeigenthümers erstreckt sich auf den über dem Grunde befindlichen Raum und—soweit das Bergbaugesetz nicht anderweitig verfügt — auf den darunter befindlichen Erdraum: der Eigenthümer ist jedoch verpflichtet diejenigen Einwirkungen zu dulden, welche in solcher Höhe resp. Tiefe stattfinden, dass seine Interessen dadurch nicht verletzt werden.

CODE CIVIL ITALIEN (traduction Prud'homme), art. 440.

> Celui qui a la propriété du sol a également la propriété de l'espace au-dessus du sol et de tout ce qui se trouve au-dessus et au-dessous de la superficie.

SCHWEIZERISCHES ZIVILGESETZBUCH 1907, Art. 667.

> Das Eigentum an Grund und Boden erstreckt sich nach oben und unten auf den Luftraum und das Erdreich, soweit für die Ausübung des Eigentums ein Interesse besteht.

KANTONALE RECHTE. See Huber, System und Geschichte des Schweiz. Privatr. 1889 III, pag. 238.

CODE CIVIL ESPAGNOL (trad. A. Levé), art. 350.

> Le propriétaire d'un terrain est le maître de ce qui est au-dessus et de ce qui

Le droit de jouissance du sol s'applique non seulement au sol lui-même dans toute sa profondeur, sauf les dispositions de la loi relative aux mines, mais encore à l'espace aérien qui surmonte ce sol, jusqu' à la hauteur où cet espace est susceptible d'être occupé.

CODE CIVIL DE L'EMPIRE DU JAPON (trad. Montono et Tomii), art. 207.

La propriété du sol emporte, sous réserve des restrictions apportées par les lois et ordonnances, la propriété du dessus et du dessous.

CODE CIVIL MUSULMAN (trad. Meysonnasse), art. 175.

La propriété du sol emporte la propriété du dessus et du dessous.

————————

2. Literature concerning the Extent of Land-property.
(See p. 34—37).

PORTALIS. Code civil suivi le l'exposé des motifs. 1820. IV, pag. 38.

On comprend que la propriété serait imparfaite si le propriétaire n'était libre de mettre à profit pour son usage toutes les parties extérieures et intérieures du sol ou du fonds qui lui appartient, et s'il n'était le maître de tout l'espace que son domaine renferme.

THÉOPHILE HUC. Commentaire théorique et pratique du Code civil. 1893. IV, pag. 162.

La loi commence par déclarer que la propriété du sol emporte la propriété du dessus. Cela signifie que l'espace aérien situé au-dessus d'un fonds, est la propriété exclusive de ce fonds.

BAUDRY—LACANTINERIE. Traité théorique et pratique de droit civil. 1899. V, no. 331.

Le propriétaire du sol n'a pas seulement la liberté d'élever des constructions, de faire des plantations, mais le droit exclusif qu'il possède sur la colonne d'air située au-dessus de son fonds lui permet aussi d'arrêter les empiètements des tiers sur ce domaine aérien.

AUBRY ET RAU. Cours de droit civil français. 1897. II, § 192.

Le propiétaire d'un terrain est propriétaire de l'espace aérien au-dessus du sol.

DALLOZ. Jurisprudence générale. Recueil périodique. 1900, 2, 362.

...l'espace aérien, c'est-à-dire la partie utilisable existant au-dessus du sol, ne peut comme étant compris dans la propriété du sol, être utilisé sans l'autorité du propriétaire.

J. LAURENTIE. Le domaine aérien. Revue du Tourisme et des Sports 15 déc. 1908, pag. 265.

En principe le propriétaire de la moindre parcelle terrain est propriétaire de la masse terrestre située entre la surface de son terrain et le centre de notre planète et de l'espace situé au-dessus de son fonds jusqu' aux dernières limites de l'atmosphère,

PASSION. La Revue Aérienne 10 avr. 1909, pag. 203.

Le propriétaire du sol est propriétaire des enfers jusqu' au ciel.

JULIEN CIRIER. Du délit de chasse sur le terrain d'autrui. Douai 1887, pag. 141.

La propriété du dessous emporte selon moi en matière de chasse, celle du dessus; les fonds ne sont plus limités par les lignes tracées à la surface, mais par des plans verticaux passant par ces lignes.

CH. JULLIOT. De la Propriété du Domaine aérien. 1909, pag. 17.

De par la volonté de la loi, vous êtes propriétaire, jusqu à l'infini, de l'espace géométrique assis sur votre sol.

NAQUET. See Julliot l. c. pag. 12.

M. Naquet ne peut admettre l'union et l'incorporation de l'espace avec le sol sans un lien corporel, plantation ou construction, qui ne peut exister qu' à l'égard de choses qui se fixent sur le sol.

MARCEL PLANIOL, Traité élémentaire de droit civil. 1901. I, pag. 377.

Laissons de côté ce qui est dessus! C'est l' objet de la théorie de l'accession que

bücher für die Dogmatik des heutigen römischen und deutschen Privatrechts. VI, pag. 21.

...so occupirt derjenige, der ein Grundstück erwirbt, nothwendig damit zugleich von dem Luftraume über demselben einen so grossen Antheil, als er zur Benutzung dieses Grundstücks nöthig hat.

R. JEHRING. Zur Lehre von den Beschränkungen des Grundeigenthümers im Interesse der Nachbarn. Jahrb. für die Dogm. des heutigen römischen und deutschen Privatr. VI, pag. 89.

Das Recht an den Luftraum oder sagen wir die Eigenthumsatmosphäre reicht nicht weiter, als das praktische Bedürfnis, das dadurch befriedigt werden soll

HESSE. Zur Lehre von den nachtbarrechtlichen Verhältnissen der Grundeigenthümer. Jahrb. für die Dogm. des heutigen römischen and deutschen Privatrechts. VI, pag. 393.

Der Luftraum gehört zum Grund und Boden in solcher Höhe, als er für die menschliche Kraft erreichbar und für das Eigenthum von Interesse ist.

DR. HEINRICH DERNBURG. Lehrburch des Preussischen Privatrechts. 1875. I, pag. 452.

Das Eigenthumsrecht am Grundstücke ergreift nicht nur dessen Oberfläche, sondern auch den Luftraum über der Fläche und das Unterirdische innerhalb der Gränze soweit die Möglichkeit menschlicher Herrschaft reicht.

WINDSCHEID. Lehrbuch des Pandektenrechts. 1887. I, pag. 564.

Das Eigenthumsrecht an Grundstücken erstreckt sich auf den unter und über dem befindlichen Raum.

Dr. F. MEILI. Das Recht der modernen Verkehrs- und Transportanstalten. 1888, pag. 123.

Das Eigentum steigt zum Himmel empor und geht in die Tiefe in direkter Linie von der Oberfläche zum Centrum der Erde. Allein dieser Satz muss modifiziert werden, da die Romantik nicht in das Recht hinein hört.

Dr. P C. PLANTA. Bündnerisches Civilgesetzbuch mit Erläuterungen. 1863, pag. 127. Bei Grundstücken erstreckt es (das Eigenthum) sich auch auf den Luftraum über und auf den Boden unter demselben, so weit jener und dieser dem Eigenthümer nutzbringend sein können.

EUGEN HUBER. System und Geschichte des Schweizerischen Privatrechts. 1889. III, pag. 238.

Zunächst betreffend den Körperumfang eines Immobile innerhalb bestimmter Grenzen ist zu sagen, das unsre Rechte der allgemeinen Lehre folgen und dem Eigenthümer ein Eigenthum an Grund und Boden in die Tiefe und an der Luftsäule in die Höhe ohne bestimmte Grenzen zuerkennen.

C. WIELAND. Kommentar zum Schweizerischen Zivilgesetzbuch von Egger, Escher, Reichel, Wieland. 1909. IV, ad art. 667.

Manche kantonalen Rechte gewähren dem Eigenthümer, der älteren Rechtsauffassung entsprechend, die Herrschaft nach der Höhe und nach der Tiefe in unbeschränkter Ausdehnung. . . . Das Z. G. B. beschränkt den Herrschaftsbereich des Eigenthümers mit Rücksicht auf sein Interesse . . . . Darüber hinaus kann er die Inanspruchnahme des Raumes über und unterhalb der Grundfläche nicht verbieten, z. B. Anlage von elektrischen Leitungsdrähten über den Luftraum, durchfliegende Luftballons. Je nach der Zweckbestimmung des Grundstückes kann demnach der Umfang des Eigentums nach der Höhe und nach der Tiefe verschieden sein.

Dr. JOSEF SCHEY. Taschenausgabe des österr. B. G. B. (herausgegeben von der Manz-schen K. u. K. Hof-Verlags-und Universitäts Buchhandlung Wien), ad § 297.

Die Luftsäule über einem Grundstücke gehört zu diesem, soweit eine Herrschaft über sie möglich ist.

communis omnium, beide also nicht Eigentumsgegenstand; nur ist freie Verfügung über den senkrecht über dem Grundstück befindlichen Lufraum bis in die erforderliche Höhe ein notwendiges Mittel der Ausübung des Grundeigentumes selbst; nur dieses Verfügungsrecht kann gemeint sein in § § 297, 422 etc.

THOMAS BRETT. Commentaries on the present laws of England. 1891, pag. 2.

Land in its legal signification comprehends not only the land itself, but also all that is above the soil—castles, houses and other buildings, water, forests and trees .... The maxim of the law on this subject is cujus est solum, ejus est usque ad coelum et inferos.

SIR WILLIAM BLACKSTONE. The commentaries on the laws of England. 1876. II, pag. 15.

Land hath also, in its legal signification, an indefinite extent, upwards as well as downwards. Cujus est solum ejus est usque ad coelum, is the maxim of the law.

STEPHEN. Stephen's commentaries on the laws of England (partly founded on Blackstone) 1903. I, pag. 94.

Land hath also, in its legal signification, an indefinite extent, upwards as well as downwards. Cujus est solum ejus est usque ad coelum, is the maxim of the law, upwards .... So that the word "land" includes not only the face of the earth, but everything under it and over it.

SIR FREDERICK POLLOCK. The Law of Torts, pag 332.

It does not seem possible on the principles of the common law to assign any reason why any entry above the surface should not also be a trespass, unless indeed it can be said, that the scope of possible trespass is limited by that of effective possession.

F. B. BADEN-POWELL. Law in the air. The National Review. March 1909, pag. 78.

It has recently been pointed out by lawyers, that according to law an Englishman's property extends upwards to the skies.

THE LAW JOURNAL. Jan. 16, 1909, pag. 27. The control of the air.

The maxim Cujus est solum, ejus est usque ad coelum has been taken over from the Civil Law by us, and may be said to be, in a modified degree, a maxim of English Law .... That, apart from any question of the space above being actually owned by some other private person, a landowner cannot claim the complete ownership of the space in an upward direction to an indefinite extent, may be taken to be settled law. The difficulty is to define the boundary of his ownership with sufficient precision.

THE SOLICITORS' JOURNAL AND WEEKLY REPORTER. Sept. 28. 1907, pag. 771. Airships a legal Problem.

If the right to the enjoyment of the column of air above a piece of land were no longer to be regarded as in the nature of a proprietary right, but as a right to the enjoyment of the column of air without such interference as would amount to a nuisance, ... Under this principle actual ownerschip might be held to extend only to so much of the column of air above the land as was necessary for the use of buildings erected on the land, whilst the owner would be entitled to restrain (as a nuisance) anything amounting to improper interference with his enjoyment of the upper part of the air.

REEVES. Real Property. I, pag. 113.

I can restrain my neigbor from swinging his shutters out over my roof; and he who without permission, digs into my soil a thousand feet below the surface, or stretches a telegraph or telephone wire over it, or flies in an airship thousands of

It (the land) has an indefinite extent upwards as well as downwards so as to include everything terrestrial under or over it.

JAMES KENT. Commentaries on American Law. 1896. III, pag. 401 [621].

Corporal hereditaments are confined to land, which, according to Lord Coke, includes not only the ground or soil, but . . . . has an indefinite extent upwards as well as downwards, so as to include everything terrestrial, under or over it.

WORDS AND PHRASES. V, pag. 3975.

It is elementary that land itself, in legal contemplation extends from the sky to the depths.

W. ARCHIBALD MC. CLEAN. The Evolution of a Legal Sky Pilot. The Green Bag. July 1904, pag. 464.

When man flies, whither he listeth, there may have to be a radical change, or at least some modification in that old maxim, he who owns the soil owns it up to the sky . . . . We venture to predict, that the law will never recognise any right of recovering for trespassing through my air shaft unless actual damage results therefrom.

LAND. Verklaring van het Burgerlijk Wetboek. 1889. III, pag. 107.

ad art. 626a.

. . . . he (the lawmaker) lays down the rule, that the property of the soil includes anything united with the soil, in or on it.

MR. C. W. OPZOOMER. Het Burgerlijk Wetboek verklaard. 1871. III, pag. 214.

It (the law) lays down the principle that the property of land includes anything on and in the land, that is in such a way on and in (or under) the soil, that it is one with it.

MR. C. ASSER. Handleiding tot de beoefening van het Nederlandsch Burgerlijk Recht. 1896. II, pag. 62.

His property extends in a sense without any limit in the vertical direction. This principle which is to be found in every civil law, is sometimes referred to by expressions such as: „Cujus est solum ejus est usque ad coelum," etc.

Same book, reviewed by MR. PAUL SCHOLTEN. 1905, pag. 76.

. . . . it seems to us that the decision of the Court saying that the property of land includes the right to the enjoyment of the airspace above the land, but that this right extends but as far as is necessary for the use of the land, is still the right one.

MR. G. DIEPHUIS. Het Nederlandsch burgerlijk recht. 1880. VI, pag. 32.

It (art. 626a) has taken the place of art. 552a C. N. "la propriété du sol emporte la propriété du dessus et du dessous". Does one mean by "dessus" and "dessous" only what is built on the land or in any other way united with it? This seems the less probable because of art. 553 and the following treating on this subject. The meaning must be that the proprietor of the soil has the disposition of anything under or over it.

S. J. FOCKEMA ANDREAE. Beschouwingen over Burenrecht. Leiden 1868, pag. 44.

The use (of the soil) would often be difficult or even impossible, if the space above the land was not unoccupied. So, whenever it is occupied, the possibility of use being attacked thereby, the proprietor is entitled to prevent such occupation in virtue of the right which guarantees that possibility, in virtue of his right of property.

MR. LEVY. Het sprookje van de luchtkolom, II. De Amsterdammer, 23 Sept. 1884.

Intact be the right of the proprietor to dispose of the airspace above his land, accor-

grafen en telefonen. Groningen 1885, pag. 32.

We may conclude therefore that also according to our civil code the proprietor of land has an unlimited and exclusive right to the space under it and over it and that he is not obliged to tolerate any interference with that space.

MODDERMAN. Tijdschrift voor het Nederl. Regt. III, pag 16.

One must simply give the proprietor in virtue of his right of land-property, the right to use the air above him, as he needs it.

J. E JACOBSON. De Telefonie van privaatrechtelijk standpunt bezien. Amsterdam 1893. pag. 13.

These words of Modderman (see former reference) constitute also the basis of our opinion.

3. Articles of Laws concerning the Toleration of Aerial Electric Wires (see p. 37).

NETHERLANDS.

Law to regulate communication by means of electro-magnetic telegraphs. 7th March 1852. Off. Gaz. 48.

Art. 4. The proprietors of land over or through which an electro-magnetic telegraph is laid, without there being reason to expropriate, are bound to tolerate the placing of the necessary poles, the stretching of the wires over or under the ground and whatever there may be necessary for the maintenance of the telegraphs.

Law concerning the construction, exploitation and use of telegraphs and telephones, 11th Jan. 1904. Off. Gaz. 7.

Art. 7. Without prejudice to art. 4, every one is obliged to tolerate the construction and maintenance of telegraph and telephone wires over public and other grounds, buildings and waters, but without any fixture or contact and under reservation of the owner's right to compensation.

FRANCE.

Loi sur les distributions d'énergie. 15 juin 1906.

Art. 12 § 2. La déclaration d'utilité publique d'une distribution d'énergie confère au concessionnaire le droit de faire passer les conducteurs d'électricité au-dessus des propriétés privées.

ENGLAND.

Telegraph Act. 1863 (26 & 27 Vict. Cap. 112).

Sec. 21. The company shall not place any work by the side of any land or building, so as to stop, hinder or interfere with ingress or egress for any purpose to or from the same, or place any work under, in, upon, over, along, or across any land or building, except with the previous consent in every case of the owner, lessee, and occupier of such land or building.

GERMANY.

Telegraphenwege-Gesetz. 1899.

§ 12. Die Telegraphenverwaltung ist befugt Telegraphenlinien durch den Luftraum über Grundstücken, die nicht Verkehrswege im Sinne dieses Gesetzes sind, zu führen, soweit nicht dadurch die Benutzung des Grundstückes nach den zur Zeit der Herstellung der Anlage bestehenden Verhältnissen wesentlich beeinträchtigt wird.

UNITED STATES.

Article VIII of the Transportation Corporation Law of the State of New-York provides for the incorporation etc. of Telegraph and Telephone Companies. Seven or more persons may become a corporation and such a corporation may erect, construct and maintain the necessary fixtures for its lines upon, over or under any of the public roads, streets and highways, and through, across, or under any of the waters within the limits of the State, and upon, through or over any other land, subject to the right of the owners thereof to full compensation.

La loi XXXI, 8/14 août 1888. (See Jacobson. De telefonie van privaatrechtelijk standpunt bezien, pag. 126; and Ann. de législ. étr. 1888, pag 492).

§ 7. Les propriétaires et possesseurs d'immeubles seront obligés de tolérer, sans droit à aucune indemnité, la suspension au-dessus de leurs inmeubles par l'entreprise et à ses frais, des lignes télégraphiques et téléphoniques, ou des signaux électriques servant à l'usage du public.

ITALY.

Legge sui Telefoni. 7 Apr. 1892.

Art. 5. I concessionari di linee telefoniche possono far passare i fili senza appoggio sia al disopra delle proprietà pubbliche e private, che dinanzi a quei lati di edifizi, ove non siano finestre od altre aperture praticabili a prospetto.

Testo unico di legge sui Telefoni (Gazz. uff. del 28 Maggio 1903).

Art. 4. Idem.

SWITZERLAND.

Loi fédérale concernant l'établissement de lignes télégraphiques et téléphoniques 26 juin 1889. F. féd. III, pag. 897.

Art. 2. La confédération a sous les mêmes conditions le droit de faire passer, sans indemnité, des fils télégraphiques et téléphoniques au-dessus des propriétés privées pourvu que ces installations ne nuisent pas à l'usage auquel sont destinés les terrains ou bâtiments au-dessus desquels ces fils sont tendus.

BELGIUM.

Loi qui ouvre un crédit au département des travaux publics pour pourvoir à l'achèvement des lignes télégraphiques. 14 avr. 1852. Moniteur du 20 avr. 1852.

Art. 4. Les propriétaires et locataires des terrains ou bâtiments sur lesquels ou sous lesquels le gouvernement reconnaît nécessaire d'établir une ligne télégraphique, doivent sans qu'à cet effet une dépossession puisse être exigée, tolérer le placement des poteaux, la conduite des fils tant au-dessus qu'au-dessous du sol.

Loi du 23 mai 1876, autorisant des concessions de télégraphie locale. Mon. du 28 mai 1876.

Art. 5 idem.

Loi concernant l'établissement et l'exploitation de réseaux téléphoniques. 11 juin 1883. Mon. du 12 juin 1883.

Art. 4. Les propriétaires et occupants sont tenus de tolérer au-dessus de leurs bâtiments ou terrains les fils des lignes téléphoniques régies par la présente loi, mais sans attache ni contact.

LOUISIANA.

Act no. 124. 1880 (Ann. de législ. étrang, X, pag. 689).

Les compagnies, légalement établies, ayant pour objet la transmission rapide des nouvelles par le télégraphe, le téléphone ou autre système du même genre, peuvent, aux termes de l'„act" no. 124 faire passer leurs fils sur ou le long de toute propriété publique ou privée.

4. Jurisprudence (p. 40—43).

A. Pro.

1. Unconditionally.

NETHERLANDS.

Court of Amsterdam 27th Nov. 1883 (W. 5023).

The stretching of wires is an encroachment upon the legal right of the proprietor to dispose of the space above his land and constitutes an unlawful interference, which the proprietor is not obliged to tolerate.

Supreme Court 29th Jan. 1894. (W. 6468).

Request of att. gen.

. . . . and that the expression „ground" does not mean only the surface of the globe is proved by art. 626 c. c., saying in somewhat different terms the same as the old adage: "Cujus est solum ejus est usque ad coelum", and as art. 552 C. N.: "la propriété du dessus emporte la propriété du dessus et du dessous".

Judgment.

. . . that art. 641 c. c. gives the proprietor the exclusive right to appropriate the game on his grounds, that this expression is large, so as to include not only the animals touching the ground but also the birds flying over it. . . .

Court of Heerenveen 24th Jan. 1896. (W. 6780).

Conclusion publ. pros. (judgment conform).

.., then perhaps with a view to art. 626 c. c. the question might arise wether one can call the possession untroubled and unequivocal since the possessor of the ground and the air above it. . . .

Supreme Court 24th Dec. 1902. (W. 7849).

Considering that the plaintiff, having the right (of property) as to the said land, is entitled according to art. 626 c. c. to erect on that land any plantings and buildings he likes to, whereas art. 728 affirms explicitly that he is entitled to build on his ground as high as he wants;

Considering that this right of the plaintiff as proprietor of the land has been interfered with by the defendant's stretching and maintaining telephone wires over that land;

Considering, that . . . the unlawfulness of the defendant's act can only depend on the existence of the right of property of the plaintiff and not on his exercising this right. . . .

FRANCE.

Trib. corr. d'Arras 1828, Gaz. Trib. 30 oct. 1828 (Julliot, l. c. pag. 10).

Tirer sur un gibier qui se trouve au-dessus d'un terrain où l'on n'a pas le droit de chasse, constitue un délit de chasse.

Cour de Paris 15 avr. 1864, Dalloz 1880. 3. 103.

Trib. civ. de Corbeil 10 déc. 1880 (Cirier, l. c. pag. 143).

Le fait de tirer au vol n'est licite que si l'oiseau est en deça de la ligne verticale fictive qui sépare les deux propriétés.

Trib. civ. de Tours 19 juin 1887, Dalloz 1900. 2. 361, note a.

Que rien dans notre législation ne limitant ou ne réglementant le droit du propriétaire sur le dessus de sa propriété, on doit donc en inférer que son droit peut s'étendre à une hauteur indéterminée et suivant sa volonté.

Cour d'appel d'Amiens 19 févr. 1896, Dalloz 1896. 2. 464.

. . . . le droit de propriété s'étendant aussi bien au-dessus du sol qu'à sa surface . . . Tirer sur un gibier qui se trouve au-dessus d'un terrain où l'on n'a pas le droit de chasse, constitue un délit de chasse.

Trib. de paix de Lille 15 nov. 1899, Dalloz 1900. 2. 361.

Attendu qu'il n'existe aucune loi qui, par dérogation à l'art. 552 C. c. autorise les compagnies d'éclairage électrique à faire passer leurs câbles ou fils au-dessus des propriétés privées . . . .

Cour d'appel de Lyon 9 avr. 1903, Dalloz 1906. 2. 178.

. . . qu' au moment où il a tiré ses deux coups de fusil, les canards se trouvaient encore au-dessus de la Saône, d' où ils venaient de se lever; que par ce seul fait le délit reproché au prévenu aurait bien été commis . . .

BELGIUM.

Cour d' appel de Bruxelles 31 mai 1876, La Belg. jud. 1876, pag. 602.

. . . qu' il est de règle que la propriété du dessous emporte la propriété du dessus et que cette règle est appliquée en matière de chasse en ce sens que le propriétaire du dessous au son ayant-droit a seul le droit de s'approprier le gibier qui plane au-dessus de son terrain.

SWITZERLAND.

Bundesgerichtliche Commission (Meili, Die Anwendung der Expropriation auf die Telephonie 1888, pag. 50).

Für die blosse Duldung der Telephondrähte über dem Luftraume in einer Distanz von 2.30 M. bis 3.05 M. über der Zinne in Verbindung met einem exceptionnellen Tretrechte würde als angemessen bezeichnet . . .

ENGLAND and UNITED STATES.

Lemmon v. Webb, 70 L. T. 275.

. . . some of the branches of which overhang the land of the other, what is the right of that other as regards those branches, which certainly interfere with his property, that is to say, with something between heaven and earth belonging to him.

Clifton v. Viscount of Bury and others, 4 T. L. R. 8.

. . . the traversing of the land by the bullets in the use of the 1000 yards range was not unattended with risk, and certainly it would cause a not unreasonable alarm, which rendered the occupation of that part of the farm less enjoyable than the plaintiff was entitled to have it. His Lordship was satisfied therefore, that the plaintiff had a legal grievance sufficient to enable him to maintain an action... As regards the claim for injunctions, his Lordship thought he ought to grant them as prayed against all the defendants to prevent the future use of the 1000 yards range in such manner as to cause bullets fired along it to traverse the land of the plaintiff.

National Telephone Co. v. Baker, 62 L. J. ch. 699. (Engineering June 11, 1909 pag. 793).

or to an injunction, or to damages in condemnation proceedings, if a telegraph or telephone company stretches its wires over his lands.

Finchly Electric Light Co. v. Finchley Urban District, 1902, 1 Ch. 866; 1903, 1 Ch. 437. (Solicitors' Journal and Weekly Reporter 51, pag. 771).

The landowner is entitled to prevent an electric wire being stretched across his land.

Kenyon v. Hart, 34 L. J. M. C. 87 (Engineering l. c.).

That raises the old query of Lord Ellenborough (Pickering v. Rudd, 4 Camp. 219) as to a man passing over the land of another in a balloon; he doubted whether an action for trespass would lie for it. I understand the good sense of that doubt, though not the legal reason of it.

Murphy v. Bolger, 60 Vt. 723.

It therefore (because land has an indefinite extent upwards as well as downwards) follows that one is liable in an action of ejectment for a projection of his roof over another's land.

Hoffman van Armstrong, 48 N. Y. 201.

The owner of land commits no tort if he cuts off the limbs of trees overhanging his land, though the trees themselves grow upon the land of another, since he is entitled to a free approach to his land from above. (See also Grandona v. Lovdal, 78 Cal. 611).

---

2. Conditionally.

NETHERLANDS.

Court of appeal of Amsterdam, 18 Oct. 1901. (W. 7682).

Considering that the right of property of the defendant in appeal is not conceivable as a useful right unless he is entitled to move in the space above his land and to perform there anything — under reservation of the rights of thirds and of restrictions by public law — he thinks desirable for the use of the soil, and to prevent therefore thirds to interfere with that airspace, ... that, this being so, the said right does not necessarily include a right and enjoyment of that space as exclusive as the right concerning the land, but only to such an extent as is demanded by the use and enjoyment of the land.

FRANCE.

Cour de Douai 8 juin 1887, Dalloz 1896. 2. 464. (Julliot, l. c. pag. 11.)

Attendu que si l'air en tant qu' élément est une chose non susceptible d'appropriation individuelle, il est hors de conteste que, en tant qu 'espace, dans la limite où il est utilisable, il est attribué par la loi, notamment par les art. 552 et 672 du C. c. au propriétaire de la surface.

Trib. civ. de Compiègne 19 déc. 1888, Dalloz 1900. 2. 361, note b.

..... que la propriété du sol doit nécessairement entraîner celle de la partie utilisable existant au-dessus de ce même sol.

Trib. civ. de la Seine 7e ch. 19 mai 1908, Le Droit 24 oct. 1908 (Bonnefoy, l. c. pag. 125).

Attendu que la propriété du sol emporte celle du dessous et du dessus y compris l'espace aérien utilisable.

Pickering v. Rudd, 4 Camp. 219. (Engineering, June 11, 1909, pag. 793).

But I am by no means prepared to say, that firing across a field in vacuo, no part of the contents touching it, amounts to a tresspass. Nay, if this board over-hanging the plaintiff's garden be a tresspass, it would follow that a aeronaut is liable to an action of trespass at suit of the occupier of every field over which the balloon passes in the course of his voyage .... If any damage arises from the object which overhangs the close, the remedy is by an action on the case.

Butler v. Frontier Telephone Co. N. Y. Court of Appeals, 186 N. Y. 486.

Within reasonable limitations land includes not only the surface but also the space above and the part beneath. Usque ad coelum is the upper boundary and while this may not be taken too literally, there is no limitation within the bounds of any structure yet erected by man... According to fundamental principles and within the limitations mentioned, space above land is real estate the same as the land itself. The law regards the empty space as if it were a solid, inseparable from the soil and protects it from hostile occupation accordingly.

GERMANY.

Reichsgericht Civ. Sen. 21 Sept. 1898, Entsch. des Reichsger. 42, pag. 205.

Klägerin ist daher für berechtigt zu erachten, die Beseitigung von Leitungen, welche seitens des Beklagten über ihre Strassen und Plätze geführt worden sind, zu verlangen, und die künftige Ueberspannung der Strassen und Plätze von ihrer Genehmigung abhängig zu machen, vorausgesetzt dass die Drähte der Ausnutzung ihres durch den Strassenverkehr beschränktes Eigentumes hinderlich oder lästig sein können.

Reichsger. Civ. Sen. 29 Okt. 1904, Entsch. der Reichsger. Neue Folge, IX, pag. 116.

Mit Recht versteht der Ber. Richter § 905 Satz 2 dahin, dass die damit eingeführte Beschränkung des Eigentumsrechts erst beginnen soll wo jedes Interesse des Eigen-tümers an der Ausübung von Eigentumsrechten oberhalb der Oberfläche seines Grundeigentums aufhört.

AUSTRIA.

O. G. H. 27 Nov. 1907 (Österr. Zentralbl. für die juristische Praxis, Jänner 1909 pag. 33).

Der senkrecht über dem Grundstücke sich erhebende Luftraum gehört zu demselben nur in soweit, als eine Herrschaft über ihn möglich ist; der Besitz des Luftraums erstreckt sich somit nicht weiter, als von demselben Gebrauch gemacht werden kann, als das praktische Bedürfnis reicht, das dadurch befriedigt werden soll.

Electric Telegraph Company v. Overseers of Salford, 11 Ex. 181.

The posts and wires placed by a Telegraph Company along a line of railway con-stitute an occupation of land which renders the Company rateable in respect of the land covered by the posts as well as the land covered by the wires.

Lancashire Telephone Company v. Manchester Overseers. C. A. 14 Q. B. D. 267.

Ambrose. Q. C.:

It appears from the case that the two ends of the wire are fixed, the one on the appellants' own premises and the other on the premises of the subscriber, and by the wire which goes overhead the appellants occupy so much of the land as the wire covers—just as much as water and gas companies occupy land by their

NETHERLANDS.

    Supreme Court. 22th Dec. 1882 (W. 4861).

    Conclusion att gen. (judgment conform).

    . . . . professor Opzoomer has, in my opinion with good reason, defended the thesis, that art. 626a c. c. lays down the principle that the property of the soil includes anything that is on and in the soil, in such a way that it is united with it.

    Local Court of Goor. 23th March 1893 (quashed Supreme Court 29th Jan. 1894, W. 6468.) Shooting at a wood cock which is above the land of a neighbor, without having permission to hunt there, is not within the reach of art. 2 of the Game Law, since "ground" can only mean the surface of the earth.

FRANCE.

    Cour de Douai 11 févr. 1880, Dalloz 1896, 2. 464.

    Tirer sur un gibier qui se trouve au-dessus de la propriété d'autrui ne constitue pas un délit de chasse.

BELGIUM.

    Cour d'appel de Gand 6 déc. 1869, La Belg. jud. 1869, pag. 1561.

    Ne constitue pas un fait illicite de chasse commis sur le terrain d'autrui, le fait de faire lever un faisan sur son terrain et de l'abattre au moment où il planait au-dessus du terrain d'autrui.

CPSIA information can be obtained at www.ICGtesting.com
Printed in the USA
BVOW02s0049190315

392382BV00012B/98/P